ATLAS OF LANDSLIDES IN THE KYRGYZ REPUBLIC

DECEMBER 2023

Contents

Tables and Figures

Tables

Figures

Foreword

The Kyrgyz Republic has faced a myriad of disasters caused by climatological and geophysical hazards in recent years, such as landslides, earthquakes, floods, and droughts. Climate change raises the prospect that these and other natural hazards will increase in frequency and severity in the coming decades. Women and other marginalized groups face disproportionate risks from climate change and other disasters.

A comprehensive approach to landslide risk management requires enhanced systems for monitoring and management; considering engineering solutions to risks alongside nonstructural and nature-based solutions; and strengthened community awareness and engagement, particularly for marginalized groups and women. These approaches must be mainstreamed into national development strategies, policies, and investments.

This atlas provides a consolidated overview of the science, risks, and management of landslides in the Kyrgyz Republic. It draws from the national and international literature and analysis and results from the Asian Development Bank technical assistance. It covers (i) exposure and risks to key sectors; (ii) institutional arrangements; (iii) options and needs for landslide risk management; (iv) maps of landslide susceptibility, hazards, and exposure, including risk modeled of priority sites; and (v) a case study of landslide risk management in Ayu village, Osh province.

This report is targeted at professionals and the general public whose lives and work may be touched by the risks of landslides. It is presented as a high-level summary of key landslide issues and challenges in the Kyrgyz Republic. It may provide a starting point for more in-depth investigation and analysis. As Asia and the Pacific's Climate Bank, the Asian Development Bank continues to increase its support for climate and disaster resilience in its developing member countries. It is our hope that this report will be a useful resource to increase resilience in the Kyrgyz Republic.

Eugenue Zhukov
Director General
Central and West Asia Department

Foreword

Recent experience points to a steady increase in the intensity and number of natural disasters globally. Such events represent a source of profound social disruption, mass suffering, and loss of life, and as such pose a serious threat to security. This accelerated occurrence of earthquakes, landslides, mudslides, floods, fires, and other phenomena is leading to the destruction of socioeconomic assets and ecosystems.

The Kyrgyz Republic's specific rainfall patterns, mountainous relief, geological aspects, and soil and earth surface properties, as well as its high seismic hazard level, mean that it is particularly exposed to landslides. Every year, landslides cause loss of life and millions of soms of material damage to the country's economy. In the context of an increasing number of emergencies caused by natural hazards with large-scale destructive consequences, safeguarding the population and territory has become one of the important functions of the state.

Landslides in the Kyrgyz Republic cause the direct destruction of residential houses and community infrastructure; those remote in the country's gorges block river channels, leading to the formation of hazardous dammed lakes. When these burst, they can have devastating impacts on vast areas.

Meanwhile, landslide hazards are becoming ever more dangerous socially, pushing people into internal migration while subjecting them to numerous community- and household-related difficulties. Those who are unable to move out of the danger zones, or who refuse to do so, are every day at risk of being buried.

The Ministry of Emergency Situations of the Kyrgyz Republic and other concerned ministries and agencies need to make continuous efforts to increase their capacity to combat landslides. Of critical importance is the ability to actively master modern equipment and advanced technologies for use in monitoring and forecasting, as well as in strengthening landslide slopes. Special attention must be paid to training citizens on how to act in emergency situations.

B.E. Azhikeev
Minister of Emergency Situations of the Kyrgyz Republic

Acknowledgments

This atlas of landslides in the Kyrgyz Republic was prepared by the Asian Development Bank (ADB) under the technical assistance for Preparing the Landslide Risk Management Sector Project (TA 9726-KGZ) and Project Readiness Support for the Environment, Natural Resources, and Agriculture Sector in Central and West Asia (TA 6697-REG).

The report was authored by Miguel Coulier, International Centre for Environmental Management, and Andrea Tamburini, IMAGEO S.r.l., with supervision and input from Nathan Rive, Senior Climate Change Specialist of the Climate Change, Resilience, and Environment Cluster (CCRE) of ADB's Climate Change and Sustainable Development Department.

Brigitte Balthasar, Senior Disaster and Climate Risk Financing Specialist, CCRE, and Katherine Coates (consultant) provided technical review and comment. Yasmin Siddiqi, Director of the Agriculture, Food, Nature, and Rural Development Sector Office, Sector Group (SG-AFNR); Takatoshi Kawamoto, Water Resources Specialist, SG-AFNR; and Kristine Joy Obedoza, Senior Operations Assistant, SG-AFNR provided additional oversight and review. Special thanks to Anarkul Aitaliev, Director, Project Implementation Unit and Daurbek Sakyev, Director, Monitoring and Forecasting Department, Ministry of Emergency Situations, Kyrgyz Republic, for the collaboration and review.

Abbreviations

ADB	Asian Development Bank
DRR	disaster risk reduction
ICT	information and communication technology
MES	Ministry of Emergency Situations
MoES	Ministry of Education and Science
MTC	Ministry of Transport and Communications
SSCP	State System for Civil Protection
UNDP	United Nations Development Programme
UNICEF	United Nations Children's Fund
WFP	World Food Programme

Executive Summary

The Kyrgyz Republic is highly prone to landslides because of its rainfall patterns, geology, land cover, and high seismic activity.

The Asian Development Bank (ADB) is supporting the Kyrgyz Republic with $35 million in grant and loan financing for the Landslide Risk Management Sector Project. This is the first integrated preemptive landslide risk reduction investment by ADB to safeguard rural communities in the country. The project combines engineering and nature-based solutions for landslide risk reduction measures and capacity-building for institutional and community landslide monitoring and management. The project aims to reduce direct and indirect human and economic losses from landslides and safeguard ongoing development efforts.

This publication seeks to support analysis and decision-making on landslide risk management in the Kyrgyz Republic. It presents key data and maps on landslide hazards, exposure, and risk at the country and site levels.

Between 1991 and 2022, 593 landslide disaster events were recorded in the Kyrgyz Republic, resulting in 275 fatalities. There are over 4,500 landslide slopes in the country, of which about 1,200 are active and threatening over 540 settlements and 300 infrastructure assets, such as roads, energy facilities, hospitals, and schools. About 5,000 houses with a population of up to 30,000 people are under threat. Marginalized and minority groups, including women, are disproportionately at risk due to their exposure and vulnerability. Climate change is expected to exacerbate these risks.

Landslides occur across the country but with higher intensity and frequency in the south, especially across the southern Osh–Jalal-Abad region. Landslide activity in this part of the country is determined by complex interactions among tectonic, geological, geomorphological, hydrological, and meteorological factors, and human activity such as changes in land use. Landslides occur primarily in spring, with precipitation and hydrogeological processes the main triggering factors. The southern region is also the most densely populated, rural, and poor area of the country, increasing exposure and vulnerability to landslides.

Key economic sectors have suffered significant losses because of landslides. Landslides especially affect the transport, energy, and mining sectors. The impacts on other sectors, such as agriculture, education, health, water and sanitation, and services, are low in general but can be devastating locally.

The Kyrgyz Republic has a well-established institutional setup for disaster risk management and has identified key priorities on landslide risk management. The national-level State System for Civil Protection is the primary platform for emergency management. It brings together 13 government agencies and 12 specialized services with a role in emergency management. The Ministry of Emergency Situations (MES) is mandated with developing and implementing policies and programs on disaster risk management.

The government's disaster risk management strategy recognizes landslide risk as a key risk with high impact and high probability. Risk reduction and preparedness measures specific to landslides include monitoring of hazardous areas, slopes, and precipitation; early warning; resettlement; engineering works to protect settlements, businesses, and critical infrastructure; riverbank protection; improved land use; slope stabilization; and capacity-building of the population.

Since the 2000s, the government, supported by development partners and the scientific community, has implemented measures on integrated landslide risk management.

- **Landslide monitoring and risk assessment** feeds into the national early warning system. MES also maintains a register of landslides and a database to assess landslide risk. A system for post-disaster needs assessment has been established. Development partners and academic institutions have supported the adoption of new technologies for automated, real-time, and satellite-based risk assessment.

- **Physical mitigations related to landslide risk** have aimed primarily at reducing geohazards for roads and at landslide unloading. Meanwhile, nature-based solutions are becoming more popular for stabilizing landslide slopes but experience of this in the Kyrgyz Republic has primarily involved tree planting and agroforestry.

- **Resettlement** is one of the government's key measures to manage landslide risk, although there have been challenges with successful implementation. For example, resettled communities may return or refuse resettlement. Other key issues are insufficient resources, limited availability of land for cultivation, and difficulties in establishing new townships and services.

- **Education and awareness-raising** on safety and disaster risk reduction is ongoing in schools. Programming includes retrofitting, reconstructing, and rehabilitating school and preschool buildings. MES also conducts annual disaster preparedness training for heads of municipalities and community members, as well as in schools, in the communities most vulnerable to disasters.

- MES has implemented many small-scale **community-based disaster risk reduction** projects across the country, with local government as well as United Nations agencies and international and national nongovernment organizations. Activities have included community risk assessment and planning, awareness-raising, training, early warning, and facilitating national and regional coordination. Examples The database is available through an open-source platform at http://geonode.caiag.kg

- **Disaster risk financing:** The government has passed a law to establish compulsory disaster insurance for private property, which includes coverage for households against landslides. Public uptake has been limited.

Landslide atlas. Effective landslide risk management requires an understanding of where landslides have occurred or may occur; the potential affected area; the main triggers; vulnerabilities of people and assets; and potential structural and nonstructural risk management solutions. This publication presents a series of maps showing various aspects of landslide risk at national level and for a selected number of landslide sites. The maps show:

- **Landslide locations**.
- **Landslide susceptibility.** Landslide susceptibility refers to the likelihood of a landslide occurring based on an assessment of the classification, volume, or area and spatial distribution of landslides that exist or that may potentially occur.
- **Hazard.** Hazard maps represent the location, volume (or area), classification, and intensity (e.g., velocity, volume) of the potential hazard, and the probability of its occurrence within a given period.
- **Exposure.** The level of landslide susceptibility is overlaid with key assets at risk of landslides (road networks and health and school facilities).
- **Case studies in landslide modeling.** Site-specific maps present landslide hazard information for 10 landslide-prone sites in Osh and Jalal-Abad oblasts.

1. Introduction

Landslides can happen anywhere the terrain is steep or the geologic materials are weak. They can be caused by rain, earthquakes, or other factors that generate instability. As well as posing risks to human and animal life and health, they can damage or destroy buildings, roads, power lines, and other infrastructure. They can also create environmental problems such as erosion, water pollution, or habitat loss and disrupt economic activities such as agriculture, tourism, and transportation.

Landslides are recurrent natural hazards in the Kyrgyz Republic, especially in the mountainous and foothill areas. They are often triggered by intense rainfall, snowmelt, permafrost thawing, and seismic activity. Landslide activity in the country is likely becoming more intense as a result of climate change, especially rises in rainfall and temperature. It is estimated that about 30,000 people in 550 settlements across the country face immediate landslide risks.

Landslide disasters in the Kyrgyz Republic have been devastating for rural communities and key sectors such as transport, energy, and mining. In April 2017, a large landslide in Ayu village killed 24 people and destroyed 11 houses, grazing land, and parts of the only access road to the village.[1] In March 2018, a landslide cut off the drinking water supply to 18,500 people by damaging the local pipe network.[2] A massive landslide along the Dyikan–Kara-Keche road in September 2020 blocked the Kara-Keche river and destroyed power lines and the road to the biggest coal field in the country.[3]

---

[1] RFE/RL. 2017. At Least 24 Killed by Landslide in Kyrgyzstan. 29 April.

[2] A. Mokrenko. 2018. Landslide in Batken Region Leaves 350 Houses without Drinking Water. *Kyrgyz News Agency*. 19 April.

[3] D. Petley. 2021. Kara-Keche: The September 2020 Landslide in Kyrgyzstan. AGU. 28 June; Akipress. 2020. New Road to Be Built Instead of Road Blocked by Kara-Keche Landslide. 16 September.

Typical landslide above rural settlement in Kyrgyz Republic. Landslides are a frequent risk to rural communities living in the valleys of Osh and Jalal-Abad oblasts (photo by Bolot Sharshenov).

Essential to effective landslide risk management is a thorough understanding of where landslides have occurred or may occur; the potential spreading area; the main underlying triggers and how to recognize them; the characteristics of people and assets that make them more vulnerable to the impacts of landslide events; and the potential structural and nonstructural solutions to mitigate the risk.

The aim of this publication is to support the dissemination of data and information in the Kyrgyz Republic for use in planning and decision-making on landslide risk management. The key audience is the Government of the Kyrgyz Republic as well as disaster risk managers, academics, and other specialists working on landslide risk management in the Kyrgyz Republic, Central Asia, or similar mountain ecosystems.

Chapter 2 provides some technical information on landslides. Chapter 3 reviews landslide trends in the Kyrgyz Republic and impacts on key sectors; the government's institutional setup; and initiatives that have been carried out to improve the monitoring, assessment, mitigation, awareness, and financing of landslide risk in the country. Chapter 4 consists of an atlas presenting key data on landslide risk at the country level and a number of case studies. Chapter 5 presents a detailed case study illustrating the opportunities and importance of integrated landslide risk management. Chapter 6 concludes.

Landslide Risk Management Sector Project in the Kyrgyz Republic 2021–2028

The publication has been developed as part of the ongoing support of the Asian Development Bank (ADB) to the Government of the Kyrgyz Republic on landslide risk management. In 2022, ADB approved a $35 million financing package to the Landslide Risk Management Sector Project, to help reduce landslide risk in the country by deploying advanced technologies and international best practices.

This innovative project is the first integrated pre-emptive landslide risk reduction investment of ADB to safeguard rural communities in the Kyrgyz Republic. It embeds international best practices and advanced technologies to assist the country to improve risk reduction and monitoring, and combines engineering and nature-based solutions with community-based planning and capacity-building for sustainable long-term landslide safety. This will include establishing a landslide monitoring system using satellite-based radar technology and developing a gender-sensitive national landslide risk management road map.

The project will reduce the risk to communities and infrastructure from landslide events by (i) implementing landslide mitigation engineering measures, (ii) improving landslide monitoring systems, and (iii) strengthening capacity for landslide risk management.

Source: ADB. 2021. *Report and Recommendation of the President to the Board of Directors: Proposed Loan and Grant to the Kyrgyz Republic for the Landslide Risk Management Sector Project.* Manila.

2. What Are Landslides?

"Landslide" is a generic term used to describe "the downslope movement of soil, rock, and organic materials under the effects of gravity and also the landform that results from such movement."[4] The term refers to "a variety of processes that result in the downward and outward movement of slope-forming materials, including rock, soil, artificial fill, or a combination of these."[5] Landslides can be classified based on the type of movement (fall, topple, slide, spread, or flow) and the sort of material involved (rock or soil).[6]

Landslides are caused by natural factors or human activity, or a combination of both. The main natural causes are geological (weakened rock or soil material and properties, disoriented rock bed, structural discontinuity) or morphological (seismic and volcanic activity, thawing, slope saturation, glaciers, river erosion). Major human activities causing landslides are excavation or loading of the slope or base of the slope, deforestation, removal of vegetation, irrigation, mechanic vibration, or mining.

A landslide slope can be active or non-active. An active landslide slope is a slope that is undergoing or has recently undergone movement of rock, debris, earth, or soil downslope. It can be detected by means of various indicators, such as cracks, displacements,[7] deformations, or changes in vegetation or drainage patterns. An active landslide slope can be triggered or accelerated by various factors, such as rainfall, earthquakes, erosion, or human activities. A non-active landslide slope is a slope that is not undergoing or has not recently undergone movement of rock, debris, earth, or soil downslope. Such a slope can be stable or unstable, depending on the balance of forces and stresses acting on the slope. A non-active landslide slope can become active as a result of changes in the slope conditions or external factors.[8]

Countries where landslides are frequent include the People's Republic of China, the United States, Italy, Switzerland, Japan, Viet Nam, the Philippines, and Indonesia. Countries near the Himalayas, such as Nepal, Pakistan, and India, also frequently experience a high number of landslides (Figure 1).

---

[4]   L. Highland and P. Bobrowsky. 2008. *The Landslide Handbook. A Guide to Understanding Landslides*. Reston, VA: Geological Survey Circular 1325.

[5]   United States Geological Survey. 2004. Landslide Types and Processes. Fact Sheet 2004-3072.

[6]   L. Highland and P. Bobrowsky. 2008. Based on the Varnes' classification of slope movements: D. Varnes. 1978. Slope Movement Types and Processes, in R. Schuster and R. Krizek, eds, *Landslides. Analysis and Control*. Washington, DC: National Academy of Sciences.

[7]   "Landslide displacement" is the movement of soil, rock, or debris along a slope as a result of gravity, water, or other factors. Landslide Classification and Identification (accessed 8 May 2023).

[8]   X. Wang et al. 2023. Landslide Susceptibility Evaluation Based on Active Deformation and Graph Convolutional Network Algorithm. *Frontiers in Earth Science, Geohazards and Georisks*. 11; C. Song et al. 2022. Triggering and Recovery of Earthquake Accelerated Landslides in Central Italy Revealed by Satellite Radar Observations. *Nature Communications*. 13 (7278).

Figure 1: Landslide Distribution in the Central and West Asia Region

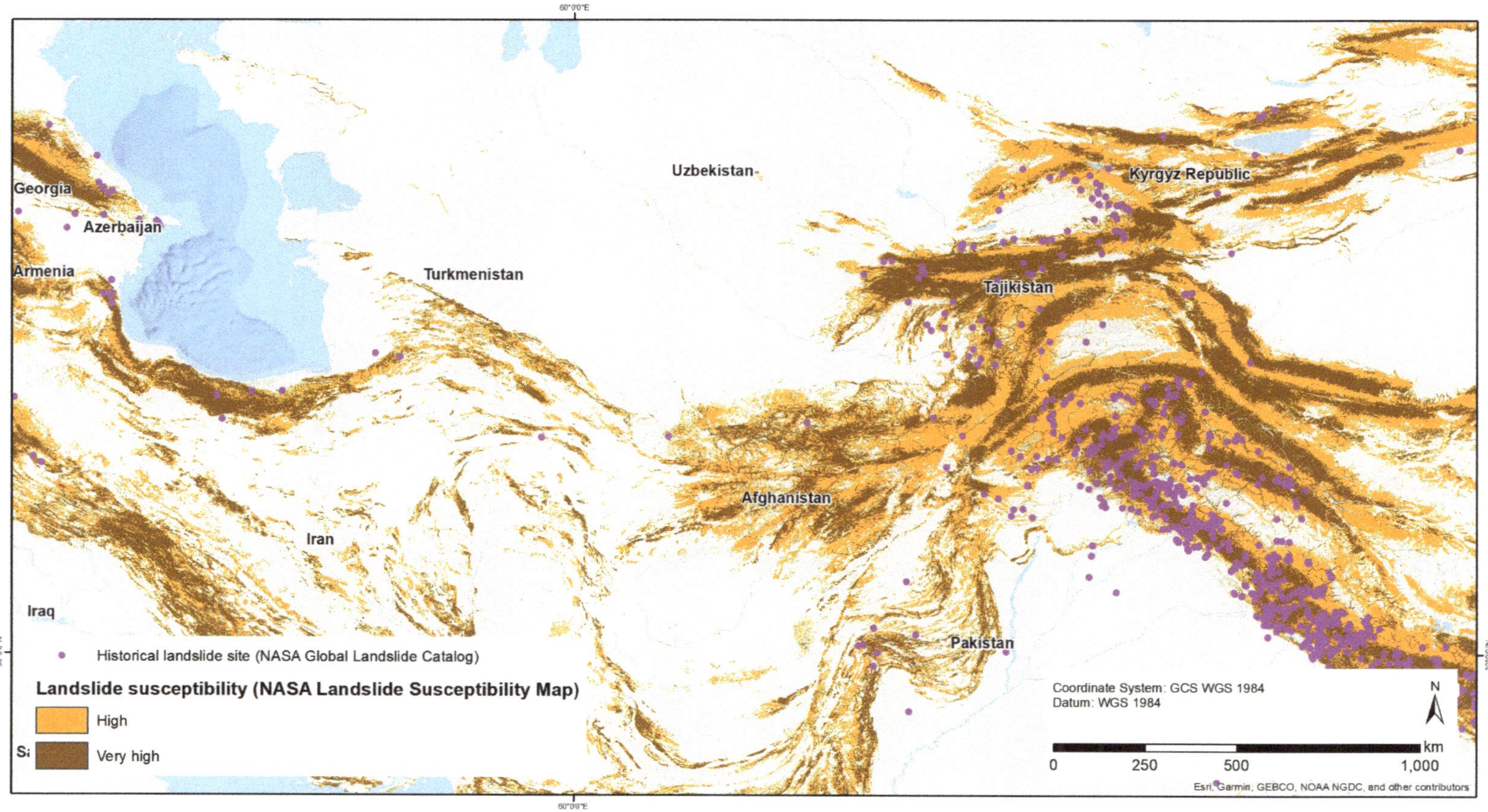

Note: Landslide susceptibility refers to the likelihood of a landslide occurring and is based on an assessment of the classification, volume, or area and spatial distribution of landslides that exist or that could occur in an area (see Section 4).

Sources: Basemap: Esri, USGS, NOAA; Historical landslide sites: NASA. Global Landslide Catalog; Landslide susceptibility: NASA Landslide Susceptibility Map.

Landslide risk can be managed or reduced in various ways. An integrated approach to landslide risk management combines structural and nonstructural measures, across sectors and at multiple scales. Such an approach is centered on the four priorities of the Sendai Framework for Disaster Risk Reduction (see Figure 2).[9]

Figure 2: Four Key Aspects of Integrated Landslide Risk Management

Source: Asian Development Bank. 2021. *Preparing the Landslide Risk Management Sector Project: Landslide Risk Assessment.* Consultant's Report. Manila.

---

[9]   United Nations General Assembly. 2015. *Sendai Framework for Disaster Risk Reduction 2015–2030.* A/RES/69/283; Asian Development Bank (ADB). 2021. *Preparing the Landslide Risk Management Sector Project: Detailed Climate Change Assessment.* Consultant's Report. Manila.

3. Landslides in the Kyrgyz Republic

The Kyrgyz Republic is highly prone to landslides as a result of its rainfall patterns, geology, soil, land cover, and seismic activity. Between 1991 and 2022, 593 landslide disaster events were recorded in the country, resulting in 275 fatalities. According to the Ministry of Emergency Situations (MES), there are 4,554 landslide slopes in the country, of which 1,186 are active and threatening over 540 settlements and 300 infrastructure assets.[10] MES estimates that about 5,000 houses with a population of up to 30,000 people are under threat of potential landslides.

Landslides occur across the country but with higher intensity and frequency in the south, especially across the Osh–Jalal-Abad region (Figure 4). Landslide activity in this part of the country is determined by complex interactions among tectonic, geological, geomorphological, hydrological, and meteorological factors, and human activity such as changes in land use. Landslides occur primarily during the rainy season in spring, as precipitation and hydrogeological processes are the main triggering factors. The southern region features some of the most populated rural areas of the country, as well as some of its poorest zones, with high exposure and vulnerability to landslides.[11]

Climate change, in particular increases in rainfall and temperature, is already resulting in an intensification of landslide activity in the Kyrgyz Republic. Climate warming, which is especially noticeable during autumn and winter, has led to an increase in the duration of the period of landslide activation in the country. Since 1985, a change in landslide recurrence period,[12,13] from long (11–13 years) to short (5–6 years) can be seen.[14] In addition, landslide displacements used to occur between March and May; in recent years, this period has started in January–February and lasted until June.[15]

---

[10] There are a total of 1,821 settlements in the Kyrgyz Republic; 540 of these (29.7%) are at risk of landslides. (Data provided by MES on 11 March 2021.)

[11] ADB. 2021. *Preparing the Landslide Risk Management Sector Project: Poverty, Gender and Social Assessment.* Consultant's Report. Manila; National Statistical Committee of the Kyrgyz Republic. 2022. Poverty Level in the Kyrgyz Republic. Bishkek.

[12] Landslide recurrence period is a statistical measure of how often a landslide of a certain magnitude or intensity occurs in a given area. For example, if the largest landslide in 100 years of record has a volume of 1,000 m³, then its recurrence period is 100/1 = 100 years. This means there is a 1% chance of a landslide of that size or larger happening in any given year. D. Peres and A. Cancelliere. 2016. Estimating Return Period of Landslide Triggering by Monte Carlo Simulation. *Journal of Hydrology. Flash Floods, Hydro-Geomorphic Response and Risk Management.* 541. pp. 256–271.

[13] Landslide recurrence period can also be used to project future landslide hazards under different climate scenarios. By using climate models to simulate the changes in extreme rainfall frequency and intensity, it is possible to estimate how landslide recurrence period will change in the future. D. Komori et al. 2018. Distributed Probability of Slope Failure in Thailand under Climate Change. *Climate Risk Management.* 20.

[14] I. A. Torgoev et al. 2008. Environmental Effects of Possible Landslide Catastrophes in the Areas of Radioactive Waste Warehousing in Kyrgyzstan (Central Asia). *In Proceedings of the First World Landslide Forum.* pp. 320–323.

[15] ADB. 2021. *Preparing the Landslide Risk Management Sector Project: Landslide Risk Assessment.* Consultant's Report. Manila.

Table 1: Decadal and Annual Physical Asset Damage from Landslide Events in the Kyrgyz Republic (Excluding Indirect Economic Loss)

Indicator	Landslide Events	Casualties	Total Physical Asset Damage from Landslide Events	
			Som (millions)	$ (millions)
Decade:				
1991–2000	221	127	–	–
2001–2010	228	105	–	–
2011–2020	142	43	107.30	1.62
Total	591	275	107.30	1.62
Year:				
2011	12	1	6.10	0.10
2012	17	0	–	–
2013	9	0	6.50	0.10
2014	3	0	–	–
2015	11	7	13.80	0.20
2016	17	1	12.50	0.20
2017	69	34	66.90	1.00
2018	4	0	1.50	0.02
2019	0	0	–	–
2020	0	0	–	–
2021	1	0	0.80	0.01
2022	1	0	1.00	0.01
Total	144	43	109.10	1.64

Source: Ministry of Emergency Situations (data provided on 11 July 2020 and updated 13 June 2023).

Note: World Bank annual and monthly averaged exchange rates have been applied to calculate the economic damage figures in US$, from World Bank. Official Exchange Rate (LCU per US$, Period Average) – Kyrgyz Republic.

The Kyrgyz Republic has suffered significant losses of lives and property as a consequence of landslides. Landslides have higher impacts on marginalized and vulnerable groups (i.e., those with low income, women-headed households, children, and older people) based on both the demographics of rural areas and the lower capacity of these groups to recover from a disaster event.[16] Besides the human toll, disasters like landslides and earthquakes are estimated to cost about 1–1.5% of gross domestic product in average economic losses.[17] Between 2011 and 2020, landslides caused physical asset damage and losses from consequent economic disruption, mortality, and morbidity of around $1.3 million (Som107,283,300). Damages from landslides are increasing, even if we exclude the year 2017, when an exceptionally high number of landslide events (69) occurred (Table 1).[18]

---

[16]   United Nations Development Programme and CAMP Alatoo. 2013. Kyrgyzstan Climate Risk Profile Bishkek.

[17]   World Bank Global Facility for Disaster Reduction and Recovery. 2015. *Country Profile: Kyrgyz Republic.* Washington, DC.

[18]   Data and information provided by MES on 11 March 2021 and updated by MES on 13 June 2023.

Impacts of Landslides on Key Sectors

Landslides affect key sectors in the Kyrgyz Republic (Table 2), especially the transport, energy, and mining sectors, and rural communities. The impacts on other sectors, such as agriculture, education, health, water and sanitation, and services, are low in general but can be devastating locally.

Table 2: Direct and Indirect Losses from Landslides in the Kyrgyz Republic by Sector

Sector type	Direct losses		Estimated indirect losses
	Economic	Human	
Transport (main roads)	Moderate	Low	High
Energy (main hydropower)	Moderate	No Data	High
Industry (mainly mining)	Moderate	Moderate	High
Rural settlements	Low	High	High
Agriculture	No Data	No Data	No Data
Education	Moderate	Low	Moderate
Health	Low	Low	Moderate
Water and Sanitation	Low	Low	Low
Services (including financial)	Low	Low	Low
ICT/telecommunications	Moderate	Low	Moderate

ICT = information and communication technology.

Note: Based on extensive literature review, expert judgment, and verification by Ministry of Emergency Situations. Direct losses refer to the total or partial destruction of physical assets, direct financial losses, or, in human terms, fatalities and injuries owing to landslide events. Indirect losses refer to the more intangible impacts of landslide events, such as impacts on trade, services provision, or the economy as a whole. Indirect losses are more difficult to measure than direct losses. (Adapted from United Nations General Assembly. 2016. Report of the Open-Ended Intergovernmental Expert Working Group on Indicators and Terminology Relating to Disaster Risk Reduction. A/71/644. 1 December.)

Source: ADB. 2021. *Report and Recommendation of the President to the Board of Directors: Proposed Loan and Grant to the Kyrgyz Republic for the Landslide Risk Management Sector Project.* Detailed Sector Assessment (accessible from the list of linked documents in Appendix 2). Manila.

Transport

The road network in the Kyrgyz Republic—with a total length of 34,800 km, including 1,400 bridges[19]—is more exposed and vulnerable to landslides than rail or air transport. The impact of landslides takes the form of both direct losses related to road and bridge repair and reconstruction and indirect losses owing to trade disruption. Trade relies heavily on road transport, which accounts for 95% of all cargo transport in the country.

---

[19]   NSC. 2017. Kyrgyzstan in Statistics. Bishkek; ARUP. 2017. Measuring Seismic Risk in the Kyrgyz Republic. Final Report for World Bank.

Landslide of 2017, Ayusai village, Osh oblast. The landslide killed 24 people and destroyed houses and community infrastructure (photo by International Centre for Environmental Management).

Landslides, rockfalls, and debris flows have often affected roads. In 2003, floods and landslides damaged 55 km of roads and destroyed or damaged 21 bridges.[20] In 2011, a large landslide in Jalal-Abad severely disrupted a section of the Bishkek–Osh highway.[21] In October 2019, a massive rockfall of about 250 m^3 in stone mass blocked parts of the Bishkek–Naryn–Torugart highway. The highway was again hit, by a 10 m^3 rockfall in November 2021 and by mudslides in July and August 2022.[22]

Energy

The energy infrastructure in the Kyrgyz Republic consists predominantly of dams, hydropower facilities, transmission infrastructure, and oil and gas pipelines. The physical infrastructure is vulnerable because of its age and inadequate maintenance. Hydropower infrastructure, producing nearly 90% of all energy in the country,[23] is especially at risk of landslides, as six of the large hydropower plants are located along the Naryn river in the high-risk Jalal-Abad region.

A potential collapse of the Dzuzumdu-Bulak landslide, which is on the right bank of the Naryn river and 5 km upstream of the Kambarata hydroelectric power plant-2 dam, could block the river flow and create a flood wave. This would endanger the hydroelectric power plant and the bridge over the Bishkek–Osh highway downstream of the dam.

[20]   N. Shimomura. 2008. *Bishkek-Osh Road Rehabilitation Projects (I) (II): Field Survey Report*. Bishkek.

[21]   *RFE/RL*. 2011. Landslide in Southern Kyrgyzstan Kills One, Blocks Highway. 12 May.

[22]   *Sputnik*. 2022. From Floods to Rockfalls – What Natural Disasters Happened in the Boom Gorge. 2 August.

[23]   CIA World Factbook. 2023. Kyrgyzstan.

Industry, Including Mining

In general, industry has low exposure to landslides, as it is mostly located in Chui region. However, the mining industry across the country, including historical uranium mining and tailing dumps, faces significant risk.[24] For instance, a landslide occurred along the Dyikan–Kara-Keche road on 14 September 2020, moving a mass of approximately 900,000 m^3, blocking the Kara-Keche river and destroying power lines and the road leading to the largest coal field in the country.[25] Kara-Keche is a village in Naryn oblast and the site of five open-cast coal mines, containing about 430 million tons of coal.

Some cities and towns, such as Mailuu-Suu, Min-Kush, Shekaftar, Sulukta, Kok-Zhangak, Chauvai, and Ak-Tuz, which are major historical mining centers, have high occurrence of landslides, caused by disturbances to slope stability as a result of mining. Mining sites such as Mailuu-Suu and nearby sites located to the northwest of Jalal-Abad city have over 200 active landslide slopes, including some with very large volumes (more than 1.0 million m^3), along with environmental hazards posed by legacy uranium mining. For example, if landslide events compromise vulnerable containment dams for tailings and dumps associated with mining sites, nearby and downstream settlements could suffer severe damage and environment impacts.

Agriculture and Rural Settlements

Agriculture accounts for 12% of the country's gross domestic product and is the main economic activity for the rural population.[26] Landslides are expected to have a low economic impact on the sector overall but they may have a significant effect on rural settlements and local productivity. Landslides can lead to the loss of crops and animals, and, in some cases, the permanent loss of agricultural land also. Rural communities are also often located in remote areas and in many cases have only one transport route linking them with regional centers. This causes additional vulnerability in terms of connectivity and access. For example, a large landslide happened in Ayu village, Osh oblast, on 29 April 2017, killing 24 people and destroying 11 houses, sections of the only access road to the village, and a large area of farmland used for grazing and hay cultivation (see Chapter 4 for a detailed case study).

Education and Health

Landslides can cause serious damage to schools, hospitals, and clinics and disrupt the services they provide. For example, a large landslide destroyed a school, a kindergarten, and a health center in Zhalpak-Tash village in Uzgen district, Osh oblast,

---

[24]　N. Komendantova et al. 2018. Industrial Development of Kyrgyzstan: Regional Aspects. IIASA Working Paper. Laxenburg.

[25]　D. Petley. 2021. Kara-Keche: The September 2020 Landslide in Kyrgyzstan; *Akipress*. 2020. New Road to Be Built Instead of Road Blocked by Kara-Keche Landslide.

[26]　63.3% were recorded as employed in agriculture, hunting, and forestry in the 2009 census (NSC. 2009. *Population and Housing Census of the Kyrgyz Republic of 2009, Book I: Main Social and Demographic Characteristics of Population and Number of Housing Units*. Bishkek).

on 23 April 2017. In 2003, heavy rain triggered floods and landslides damaged 32 schools in the oblasts of Chui, Jalal-Abad, and Osh.[27]

In 2013, 86% of schools in the country were rated as having low structural integrity because of their age, construction materials, and lack of maintenance, increasing their vulnerability to disasters.[28] Many health facilities suffer from a lack of maintenance and predate current building norms, as well as having nonstructural deficiencies.[29] A countrywide seismic risk assessment in 2017 estimated that seismic events could cause annual economic losses of $6 million–$12 million for schools and $27 million–55 million for health facilities, as well as killing 32–54 teachers and students every year.[30]

Water and Sanitation

Water and sanitation systems are not widely present in the areas most affected by landslides, so damage to physical infrastructure is low at the national level but high at the local level. For example, a landslide in Osh oblast on 27 March 2018 damaged the pipe network and temporarily cut off the drinking water supply to 18,491 people. A landslide in Batken oblast on 19 April 2018 blocked a canal that supplied drinking and irrigation water to 350 families in the nearby village.[31]

Landslides and debris flows could also contaminate water sources such as reservoirs with debris and affect water quality for downstream populations. Landslides could also disrupt local water distribution networks for drinking water or agriculture.

Services

Landslides have a low economic impact on the services sector. In particular, most financial services are concentrated in urban areas, which are not prone to landslide events. However, trade, which relies heavily on road transport, may face serious disruptions. Landslides may also affect local tourism if they disrupt conditions in and access to specific sites.

Information and communication technology (ICT) infrastructure is generally more vulnerable to floods, storms, and temperature changes but unstable ground conditions and mass movements from landslides may damage above-ground components (masts, antennae, switch boxes, aerials, overhead wires, and cables) or ICT infrastructure routed along roads or bridge structures.[32]

---

[27] ADB Independent Evaluation Department. 2010. *Kyrgyz Republic: Emergency Rehabilitation Project: Validation Report.*

[28] UNICEF. 2013. *Assessment of Safety in School and Pre-School Education Institutions in the Kyrgyz Republic.* Geneva.

[29] WHO and Ministry of Health of the Kyrgyz Republic. 2017. Report on the Results of a Hospital Safety Assessment in the Kyrgyz Republic. Bishkek.

[30] Although damage from landslides is also expected to be significant, the study did not include risks from seismically triggered landslides (ARUP. 2017. Measuring Seismic Risk in the Kyrgyz Republic). The study informed the government's ongoing Safer Schools Program, which is carrying out selected seismic retrofits and functionality upgrades for high-priority schools (World Bank Global Facility for Disaster Reduction and Recovery. 2019. *Safety Prioritization of School Buildings for Seismic Retrofit using Performance-Based Risk Assessment in the Kyrgyz Republic.* Washington, DC).

[31] A. Mokrenko. 2018. Landslide in Batken Region Leaves 350 Houses without Drinking Water.

[32] L. Horrocks et al. 2010. Adapting the ICT Sector to the Impacts of Climate Change. Final Report. London.

Government Priorities on Landslide Risk Management

The Kyrgyz Republic has a well-established institutional setup on disaster risk management and has identified key priorities, especially on landslide risk management.

Key Institutions

The national-level State System for Civil Protection (SSCP), established on the foundations of the Soviet civil defense system, is the primary government platform for emergency management. The official mandate of the SSCP is to protect the people and territory of the Kyrgyz Republic, in peace and wartime, from natural and human-made hazards. The SSCP brings together 13 government agencies and 12 specialized services with a role in emergency management. At the national level, the prime minister is the chair of the SSCP, and the minister of emergency services is the deputy chair. At the local level, the SSCP is managed by the heads of administrative units and divisions of MES.[33]

Old landslide in Zerger village, Osh oblast. Landslides occur with higher intensity and frequency in the south of the country due to its geology and seismic activity (photo by International Centre for Environmental Management).

---

[33] ICF Consulting Services. 2016. Disaster Risk Management, Urban Planning and Housing Construction in the Kyrgyz Republic. Draft prepared for the World Bank-funded project Building Urban Resilience to Disasters in the Kyrgyz Republic. Washington, DC.

MES was formed in 2005 from the previous Ministry of Environment and Emergency Situations. **MES is mandated with developing and implementing policies and programs on disaster risk management**. Major tasks include monitoring hazards, disaster prevention, search and rescue, response and rehabilitation, and coordination at the subnational level. The activities of MES are directly funded by the central government budget.

Other key ministries and agencies involved in disaster risk management are as follows:

- The *Ministry of Transport and Communications (MTC)* is responsible for road construction and maintenance and ensuring safety on highways and roads across the country.[34] MTC's State Enterprise Design and Research Institute is in charge of road design, including the implementation of construction codes and regulations.[35] The Road Infrastructure Department is responsible for planning and undertaking monitoring and preventative/rehabilitation works regarding landslide risks.

- The *Ministry of Education and Science (MoES)*, in collaboration with other government agencies, promotes awareness of disaster risk and disaster preparedness through the training of children, students, and teachers, including on landslide risk. The Education Strategy 2012–2020 integrates disaster risk reduction (DRR), and a Safe Schools and Pre-schools in the Kyrgyz Republic in 2015–2024 program has been developed.[36]

- The *Ministry of Health* is in charge of epidemiological monitoring and disease prevention, and the provision of emergency health services, for example during and after landslides, avalanches, and disease outbreaks, as guided by the National Plan for Public Health Emergency Preparedness.[37]

- The *Ministry of Labor and Social Support and Migration* provides assistance for people affected by disasters in the form of grants and loans and works with other civil society organizations such as the Red Crescent Society in delivering emergency assistance to poor and vulnerable people. For example, in 2017, the Red Crescent Society of the Kyrgyz Republic supported 2,750 earthquake-affected people in 5 villages of Chong Alay district, Osh oblast, with tents, non-food items, medical supplies, and unconditional cash grants.[38]

- The *Ministry of Finance* has an important role in disaster response and recovery, specifically in mobilizing and allocating resources to finance post-disaster needs, identifying fiscal risk, and overseeing and monitoring budget implementation after disasters.[39] Disaster response is initially funded by the budgets of MES and

---

[34] Kyrgyz Republic Government Decree "On the Ministry of Transport and Roads of the Kyrgyz Republic" (#9 of 9 August 2016).

[35] World Bank. 2008. *Investigation and Analysis of Natural Hazard Impacts on Linear Infrastructure in Southern Kyrgyzstan*. Desk and Field Studies Report. Washington, DC.

[36] Based on a comprehensive assessment of school facilities conducted by UNICEF. MoES. Schools and Pre-Schools Safety (accessed 22 December 2022).

[37] World Bank. 2019. *Primary Health Care Quality Improvement Program (P167598). Environmental and Social Systems Assessment*. Bishkek.

[38] IFRC. 2017. *Emergency Plan of Action Final Report. Kyrgyzstan: Earthquake*. 17 November.

[39] World Bank Global Facility for Disaster Reduction and Recovery. 2019. *Safety Prioritization of School Buildings*.

local governments. If these resources are exhausted, then additional funds can be requested from the Ministry of Finance, which can make use of emergency accounts and state budget reserves and reallocate financing from other sources. In total, an estimated $60 million in reserve funds is available to support disaster response. However, this funding is not earmarked specifically for disasters.[40]

- The National Statistical Committee provides technical support to the country's damage and loss data collection and information system, with MES in charge of actual data collection.

The Kyrgyz National Platform for Disaster Risk Reduction was formally established in 2011 as a major commitment to the Hyogo Framework of Action 2005–2015.[41] It was reconfirmed in 2019 through the national disaster risk management strategy as an integral part of the government's SSCP. The platform is coordinated by MES and represents a multistakeholder national mechanism that serves as an advocate of DRR at different levels of government. Coordination with development partners is institutionalized through the Development Partners Coordination Council of the Kyrgyz Republic, which was established in 2009. The council has several working groups, including on disaster risk management and climate change adaptation and mitigation.

Priorities on Landslide Risk Management

The Concept for the Comprehensive Protection of the Population and Territories of the Kyrgyz Republic from Emergency Situations for 2018–2030 is the government's strategy on disaster risk management.[42] It recognizes the four Sendai priorities as the country's priorities on disaster risk management, listing country-specific tasks under each priority (see Figure 3).

The government's disaster risk management strategy recognizes landslide risk as a key risk with high impact and high probability. Risk reduction and preparedness measures specific to landslides emphasized in the strategy include monitoring of hazardous areas, slopes, and precipitation; early warning; resettlement; engineering works to protect settlements, businesses, and critical infrastructure; riverbank protection; improved land use; slope stabilization; and capacity-building of the population.[43]

---

40   ADB and CAREC. 2022. *Narrowing the Disaster Risk Protection Gap in Central Asia.* Manila.

41   United Nations International Strategy for Disaster Reduction. 2005. Hyogo Framework of Action 2005–2015. Kobe.

42   The Law of the Kyrgyz Republic "On Civil Protection" (#54 of 24 May 2018, updated in 2020) is the main legislative document regulating work in the field of civil defense and civil protection. The law defines the organizational and legal norms and mandates, roles, and responsibilities of the president, the parliament, the government, the authorized state body in the field of civil protection (i.e., MES), and other state bodies of executive power. It also contains procedures for emergencies and for financing civil protection activities.

43   Kyrgyz Government Resolution "Concept for the Comprehensive Protection of the Population and Territories of the Kyrgyz Republic from Emergency Situations for 2018–2030" (#378 of 30 July 2019). Chapters 9 and 10.

Figure 3: Government Priorities on Disaster Risk Management

Improving knowledge of disaster risk
- Improving the effectiveness of the monitoring and forcasting system for all type of emergencies, including the introduction of innovation technologies
- Conducting disaster risk assessment and research in the field of civil protection to improve effectiveness of disaster risk reduction measures Improving the "culture of safety" through awareness-raising and education

Improving the institutional framework for disaster risk management
- Developing a regulatory framework and organizational structure for the State System for Civil Protection
- Integrating disaster risk management in sectoral and local government plans and improvement of coordination between stakeholders
- Developing an automated control and warning system in emergency and crisis situations

Investing in disaster risk reduction measures to builde resilience
- Implementing structural and nonstructural measures to prevent emergencies and reduce the level of risk, including in the face of climate change
- Developing disaster risk insurance and social protection and encouraging domestic investments in disaster risk reduction
- Increasing disaster resilience of social facilities and infractructure

Enhancing disaster preparedness to ensure effective response
- Improving preparedness and response capacity, including of emergency services
- Developing a curriculum and training system for civil protection officials
- Improving the coordination mechanism during recovery from emergencies

Source: Kyrgyz Government Resolution "Concept for the Comprehensive Protection of the Population and Territories of the Kyrgyz Republic from Emergency Situations for 2018–2030" (#378 of 30 July 2019). Chapters 9 and 10.

Investments in Landslide Risk Management and Development Partner Engagement

Since the 2000s, the government, with support from development partners and the scientific community, has implemented numerous successful measures on different aspects of integrated landslide risk management.

Landslide Monitoring and Risk Assessment

MES' Department for Monitoring and Forecasting monitors landslides through a case-by-case review of known landslide areas based on landslide hazard assessments or after a landslide event occurs. Since 2018, the department has used unmanned aerial vehicles and geodetic instruments for monitoring.[44] The monitoring information is transmitted to the web portal of the Unified System of Integrated Monitoring and Forecasting of Emergency Situations of the Kyrgyz Republic.[45] MES also maintains

---

[44] Before 2018, monitoring was carried out mainly by means of visual observation and use of a few physical parameters.

[45] Kyrgyz Republic Government Resolution "On a Unified System of Integrated Monitoring and Forecasting of Emergency Situations in the Kyrgyz Republic" (#569 of 23 October 2019).

an annually updated register of landslides and other natural hazards, as well as a database with spatial administrative, economic, environmental, and demographic information relevant to assessing landslide risk.[46] A system for collecting data on damage and losses and a methodology for post-disaster needs assessments have also been established.

Since 2004, various development partners have supported the targeted adoption of new technologies for automated, real-time, and satellite-based hazard and landslide mapping, monitoring, forecasting, and early warning. For example, the World Bank has supported the piloting of a real-time landslide monitoring system (comprising a global positioning system, piezometers, extensometers, inclinometers, seismic monitoring stations, and a radio system); improved monitoring of hydrometeorological parameters in mountainous regions; use of mobile equipment for the monitoring of landslides; and the establishment of a web-based portal for compiling hazard monitoring information from various agencies.[47] The United Nations Development Programme (UNDP)[48] and the World Food Programme (WFP)[49] have provided hardware, software, and capacity-building support to MES crisis management centers, to strengthen and automate the government's national early warning system, including for landslides.

Major lessons from these projects include the need to invest in advanced technologies that are of low cost and easy to use and maintain, to ensure compatibility of systems, to involve communities in monitoring and early warning, and to implement ongoing institutional capacity-building.

Extensive work on mapping and assessing landslide hazard and risk, including the impact of climate change on this, has been carried out through collaboration between national and international academic institutions.[50] Over 70 landslide risk-prone sites in the south of the country have been assessed through topographic and geotechnical surveying. Hardcopy reports, including surveying results, maps, and site-specific recommendations for landslide risk management and monitoring, are available from MES.

---

[46]   The database is available through an open-source platform at http://geonode.caiag.kg.

[47]   Through the *Disaster Hazard Mitigation Project (2004–2012)*, *Strengthening Early Warning of Mountain Hazards in Central Asia (2018–2020)*, and the ongoing *Enhancing Resilience in Kyrgyzstan (2018–2024)*.

[48]   As part of *Strengthening Disaster Response and Risk Assessment Capacities in the Kyrgyz Republic and Facilitating a Regional Dialogue for Cooperation (2013–2015)* and *Strengthening Integrated Risk Governance Capacities of the Kyrgyz Republic and Regional Cooperation in Central Asia (2017–2019)*.

[49]   E. Zalkind. 2016. WFP and UK Support Disaster Preparedness in Kyrgyzstan through a Smart Application. WFP. 10 October.

[50]   Such as the Kyrgyz Complex Hydrogeological Expedition (under the State Committee for Industry, Energy, and Subsoil Use), the Institute of Seismology (under the National Academy of Science), the Scientific Engineering Centre Geopribor, the Central-Asian Institute for Applied Geosciences, the German Research Center for Geosciences Potsdam, and the University of Liège.

Physical Mitigations

Physical mitigations related to landslide risk have aimed primarily at reducing geohazards for roads and landslide unloading.[51] In 1997, 50,000 m³ of landslide mass was unloaded at the Olon-Bulak site of Kashka-Suu aiyl aimak of Aksy district, in Jalal-Abad oblast. In 2006, the World Bank's Disaster Hazard Mitigation Project used a technique called "tectonic triangle unloading" to remove 30,000 m³ of earth from the unstable top of the south side of a landslide in the Mailuu-Suu area in Jalal-Abad oblast. The major learning from these two experiences is that unloading is an effective technique to mitigate landslide risk in the Kyrgyz Republic.

On several sections of strategic roads affected by rockfalls, MTC has erected stone protective walls. In addition, a project funded by the Japan International Cooperation Agency and finalized in 2019, aimed at improving MTC's institutional capacity on mitigating the risk of geohazards such as landslides, avalanches, and rockfall on roads, supported the development of MTC's 3- to 5-year Short-Term and Mid-Term Road Disaster Prevention Management Plan. Other major project outputs were guidance manuals on risk mitigation measures to protect road assets from landslides and other hazards.[52]

Borehole drilling for geological surveys of Ayusai village, Osh oblast. Managing landslide risks may require detailed site investigations into the characteristics and depth of the landslide (photo by International Centre for Environmental Management).

---

[51]   Unloading of a landslide slope is "a process of stress relief and deformation that occurs in the rock or soil mass near the surface of a slope due to erosion, excavation or natural weathering." Unloading through excavation has to be carefully planned and executed as it can cause cracks to form and extend in the slope, weakening its strength and stability. B. Han. 2020. A New Method for Assessing Slope Unloading Zones Based on Unloading Strain. *Environmental Earth Sciences* 79. 350.

[52]   Japan International Cooperation Agency. 2019. Project for Capacity Development for Road Disaster Prevention Management in the Kyrgyz Republic. Presentation materials.

Nature-based solutions[53] are becoming more and more popular for stabilizing landslide slopes and they have, under certain conditions, fully substituted other, more traditional, gray, infrastructure solutions.[54] Experience in nature-based solutions for landslide risk management is limited in the Kyrgyz Republic, and relates primarily to tree planting and agroforestry. MES and the State Agency for Environmental Protection and Forestry have worked to promote silviculture/agroforestry along riverbanks in areas prone to erosion, mudflows, and landslides. With support from WFP, UNDP, and the Food and Agriculture Organization of the United Nations,[55] over the past 10 years over 633,440 trees and shrub vegetation items (elms, wild apples, walnuts, almonds, and roses) have been planted in 117 landslide-prone areas in Osh and Jalal-Abad, covering a total area of 1,073.76 ha.[56]

However, in the Kyrgyz Republic, the geology and geometry of landslides are often not suitable for a full nature-based stabilization, owing to the country's very deep and highly unstable loess layer. Nature-based retaining systems could be used partially for small areas, modest cuts, or retaining structures. A thorough technical feasibility analysis is always required.[57]

Resettlement

The government has managed landslide risk in some rural communities by resettling inhabitants from areas at risk, both before and after landslide events. MES has identified about 4,070 households to be resettled from disaster-prone areas, including about 3,800 households living in landslide-prone areas and about 100 households in areas prone to rockfall, as well as 170 households to be resettled temporarily.

There have been some challenges in the government resettlement experience. Resettled communities may return or refuse resettlement. This is usually because their main livelihood activity, such as livestock rearing, demands a significant land area that is not available in the new location. Other challenges are insufficient government resources, limited availability of land for cultivation throughout the country, and difficulties in establishing new townships and social services.

Learning from existing MES experience on resettlement indicates that women play a key role in restarting a life and livelihood in the new location, and also that there

---

[53] The International Union for Conservation of Nature defines nature-based solutions as "actions to protect, sustainably manage, and restore natural or modified ecosystems that address societal challenges effectively and adaptively, simultaneously providing human well-being and biodiversity benefits" (Nature-based Solutions. Accessed 29 June 2023).

[54] Under certain conditions, they have been used to stabilize very big landslides (up to 60 million m³) in environmentally sensitive areas. F. Oboni et al. 2006. Environmental Restoration of a 60M m³ Dry Asbestos Tailings Dump Using Risk Based Decision Making. CLRA 2006 Reclamation and Remediation: Policy to Practice, 31st Annual Meeting and Conference.

[55] As part of a Global Environment Fund project, Sustainable Management of Mountainous Forest and Land Resources under Climate Change Conditions (2014–2018).

[56] Kyrgyz National Platform Secretariat. 2015. National Progress Report on the Implementation of the Hyogo Framework for Action (2013-2015). Interim. Bishkek; WFP. 2019. Country Brief. Bishkek; UNDP. 2012. Green Projects for Landslide Risk Reduction in Villages of Suzak.

[57] ADB. 2021. *Preparing the Landslide Risk Management Sector Project: Technical Feasibility Study – Ayusai Subproject.* Consultant's Report. Manila.

is a need for both more community awareness on landslide risk and a dedicated government strategy and financing for resettlement.

Education and Awareness-Raising

Extensive work on safety and DRR has been carried out and is ongoing in schools, by MES with support from the United Nations Children's Fund (UNICEF)[58] and the World Bank. The Safe Schools and Pre-schools in the Kyrgyz Republic in 2015–2024 program includes detailed plans for retrofitting, reconstructing, and rehabilitating school and preschool buildings.[59]

The MES' Training and Retraining Center for Civil Protection Specialists conducts an annual disaster preparedness training program for the heads of municipalities and community members in the locations most vulnerable to disasters. The training program consists of information on potential disaster risk, DRR, disaster preparedness, and response. In addition to this, MES and MoES collaborate regularly to conduct disaster preparedness training in schools in the communities most vulnerable to disasters.

Community-based Disaster Risk Reduction

MES with local governments has implemented many small-scale community DRR projects as part of the annual Special Preventive Liquidation Measures program. These projects have implemented measures such as installing gabion boxes for riverbed and bank protection; construction and rehabilitation of protective dams and canals to reduce mudflow risk; construction and rehabilitation of bridges destroyed by disasters; and construction and rehabilitation of drainage galleries to reduce flood risk for houses. In addition, over the past 15 years, the Red Crescent Society, United Nations agencies such as UNICEF, WFP, and UNDP, and several international and national nongovernment organizations have been actively promoting community-based DRR approaches across various parts of the Kyrgyz Republic. Activities have included community risk assessment and planning, raising awareness, training, community-based early warning systems, small-scale DRR measures, and facilitating national and regional coordination.

Disaster Risk Financing

In 2015, the government passed a law to establish compulsory disaster insurance for private property.[60] To implement the law, the State Insurance Organization was set up. The insurance program covers households against fires and several disasters triggered by natural hazards, including landslides.[61] In 2019, there were 82,000 households insured under this program, and another 7,000 non-household

58   UNICEF Kyrgyzstan. Disaster Risk Reduction (accessed 29 June 2023).

59   The program has been developed based on a comprehensive disaster risk assessment. MoES. Schools and Pre-Schools Safety (accessed 22 December 2022).

60   The law was amended in 2021. Landslides remain covered under this insurance, as stated in Article 8. http://cbd.minjust.gov.kg/act/view/ru-ru/112268?cl=ru-ru

61   World Bank Global Facility for Disaster Reduction and Recovery. 2019. Disaster Risk Finance Country Note: Kyrgyz Republic. Unpublished.

insurance policies were issued. However, the compulsory property insurance covers only 9% of the country's total housing stock.[62]

The disaster risk insurance market in the Kyrgyz Republic is at a nascent stage, with few private companies. There is limited domestic technical capacity and expertise, and no use of reinsurance, which limits underwriting capacity. The State Insurance Organization is insufficiently capitalized for the number of households and range of perils it covers. Disaster data is not collected on a systemic basis for insurance purposes. There is low understanding and awareness among the public on the role and benefits of insurance for risk reduction.[63]

The World Bank is supporting disaster risk insurance in the country by improving the legal framework and by strengthening the capacity and structure of the State Insurance Organization, including through the establishment of information technology infrastructure.[64]

Regional Initiatives

The Kyrgyz Republic also benefits from multiple initiatives in the region on landslide risk management. For example, several regional projects have supported the improvement of multi-hazard forecasting and early warning systems for mountainous ecosystems.[65] In Tajikistan, the Asian Development Bank (ADB) has upgraded the early warning system for Sarez Lake, a lake formed by a major historical landslide event.[66]

The German development agency has worked with countries in Central Asia on promoting nature-based solutions for landslide risk reduction and climate change adaptation.[67] ADB is supporting countries in Central and West Asia with state-of-the-art risk assessments for the development of regional disaster risk financing mechanisms.[68] In Pakistan, ADB has piloted a nature-based solution for landslide slope stabilization,[69] generating valuable learning for the Landslide Risk Management Sector Project, including on women's empowerment in landslide risk management.[70]

---

[62] Despite the compulsory aspect and the available subsidies, the public response to this program has not been positive. The limited compensation amount does not appeal to many households, which generally expect full compensation from the government after a disaster. In addition, there is a perception that few claims will be paid out, based on previous performance of the scheme.

[63] ADB. 2021. *Report and Recommendation of the President to the Board of Directors: Proposed Loan and Grant to the Kyrgyz Republic for the Landslide Risk Management Sector Project*. Detailed Sector Assessment (accessible from the list of linked documents in Appendix 2). Manila.

[64] Through the ongoing *Enhancing Resilience in Kyrgyzstan* project (2018–2024).

[65] For example, the World Meteorological Organization/United States Agency for International Development-supported Central Asia Region Flash Flood Guidance System and the Global Fund for Disaster Reduction and Recovery's Strengthening Early Warning of Mountain Hazards in Central Asia.

[66] ADB. Tajikistan: National Disaster Risk Management Project.

[67] As part of the Enhancing People's Livelihoods in High Mountainous Regions of Central Asia through Adaptation to Climate Change project and the Transboundary Water Management in Central Asia program.

[68] As part of the Developing a Disaster Risk Transfer Facility in the Central Asia Regional Economic Cooperation Region project.

[69] ADB. Pakistan: Flood Emergency Reconstruction and Resilience Project.

[70] ADB. 2019. *Pakistani Women Plant Millions of Trees to Rebuild Climate Resilient Roads*.

4. Atlas of Landslides in the Kyrgyz Republic

This chapter presents a series of maps to visualize various aspects of landslide risk in the Kyrgyz Republic at national level and for a selected number of landslide sites. The data sources and methodologies used for the maps can be accessed in the ADB Consultant's Report on Preparing the Landslide Risk Management Sector Project: Landslide Risk Assessment (footnote 15).

The maps present different aspects of landslide risk in the Kyrgyz Republic and at site level:

- **Landslide locations.** Identified landslide locations in the country are based on two catalogs: (i) the MES catalog (Figure 4), which provides the coordinates of the center of the of the landslide mass and (ii) a catalog assembled from the academic literature (Figure 5) inferred from satellite imagery analysis with an estimation of their volumes.

- **Landslide susceptibility.** Landslide susceptibility refers to the likelihood of a landslide occurring and is based on an assessment of the classification, volume, or area and spatial distribution of landslides that exist or that may potentially occur in an area. Landslide susceptibility as shown in Figure 6 integrates the following factors recognized as the main underlying landslide triggers: morphology, geology, hydrology, precipitation, and seismic factors.[71] The maps of the most relevant input data used by the authors for the landslide susceptibility analysis are presented in Figure 7 (simplified geology), Figure 8 (average yearly precipitation), and Figure 9 (active faults, epicenters, and peak ground acceleration[72]).

- **Hazard.** Two examples of hazard maps, on landslide and mudflow, are presented in Figure 10 and Figure 11, respectively. Hazard maps represent the location, volume (or area), classification, and intensity (e.g., velocity, volume) of the potential hazard, and the probability of its occurrence within a given period.[73]

---

[71] Redrawn from H. Havenith et al. 2015. Tien Shan Geohazards Database: Landslide Susceptibility Analysis. *Geomorphology.* 249. pp. 32–43.

[72] Peak ground acceleration is equal to the maximum ground acceleration that occurred during earthquake shaking at a location. J. Douglas. 2003. Earthquake Ground Motion Estimation Using Strong-Motion Records: A Review of Equations for the Estimation of Peak Ground Acceleration and Response Spectral Ordinates. *Earth-Science Reviews.* 61 (1–2). pp. 43–104.

[73] See also MES. Monitoring and Forecasting of Hazardous Processes and Phenomenon on the Territory of the Kyrgyz Republic (in Russian).

- **Exposure.** Figure 12 and Figure 13 overlay the level of landslide susceptibility with key assets at risk of landslides: the former presents road networks and the latter villages and health and school facilities.

- **Case studies in landslide modeling.** The site-specific maps (Figure 15 to Figure 24) present landslide hazard information for 10 landslide-prone sites in Osh and Jalal-Abad oblasts (Figure 14). For each landslide site, a map with the following elements is provided:

  o Estimated landslide area;

  o Cracks identified during site surveys and other relevant geomorphological features derived from the analysis of detailed digital elevation models and drone imagery;

  o Landslide spreading area modeled with a simplified algorithm that simulates the collapse by propagating the landslide mass over the 3D model of the slope;[74] and

  o Buildings exposed to landslide hazard, obtained by applying a buffer to the estimated spreading area.

---

[74] For a detailed description of the methodology, see footnote 15.

Figure 4: Landslide Locations in the Kyrgyz Republic, Occurring over 2003–2016
(Based on the MES Landslide Inventory)

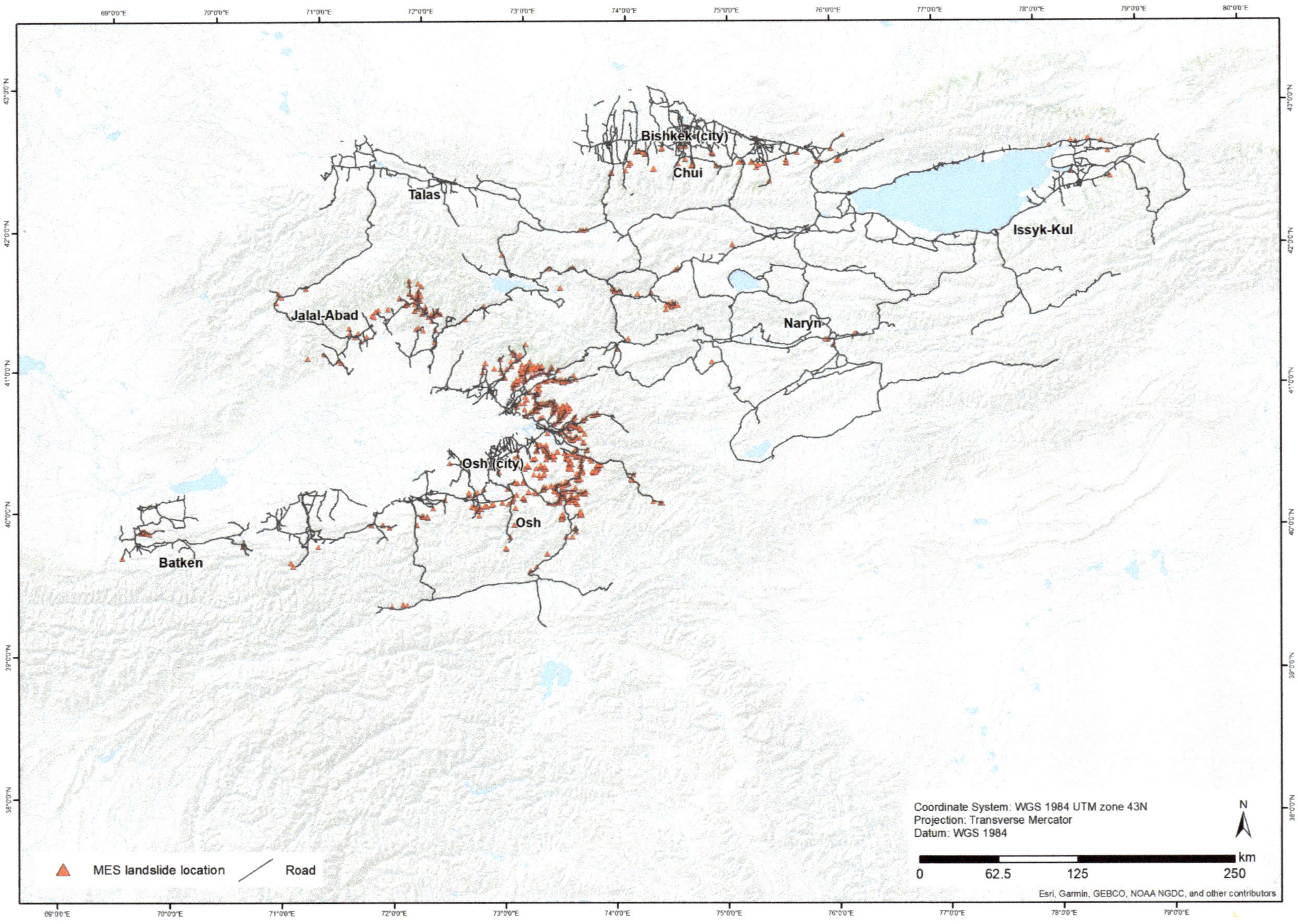

MES = Ministry of Emergency Situations.

Sources: Basemap: Esri, Garmin, GEBCO, NOAA NGDC, other contributors; Roads: OpenStreetMap; MES landslide locations: MES landslide inventory.

Figure 5: Landslide Locations in the Kyrgyz Republic
(Based on Academic Literature)

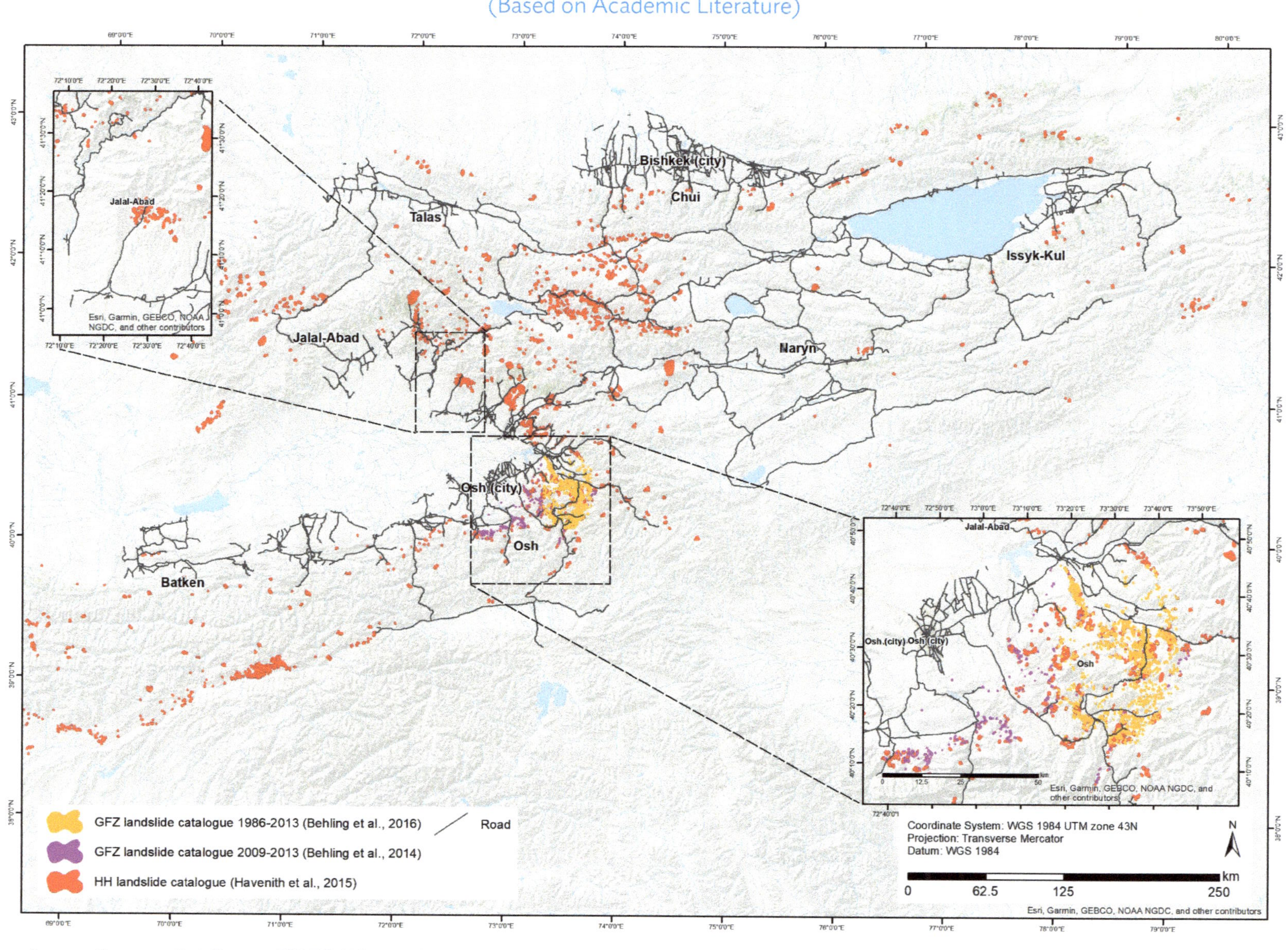

Sources: Basemap: Esri, Garmin, GEBCO, NOAA NGDC, other contributors; Roads: OpenStreetMap; GFZ landslide catalogue 1986–2013: R. Behling et al. 2016. Derivation of Long-Term Spatiotemporal Landslide Activity—a Multi-Sensor Time Series Approach. *Remote Sensing of Environment*. 186. pp. 88–104; GFZ landslide catalogue 2009–2013: R. Behling et al. 2014. Automated Spatiotemporal Landslide Mapping over Large Areas Using RapidEye Time Series Data. *Remote Sensing of Environment*. 6. pp. 8026–8055. HH landslide catalogue: H. Havenith et al. 2015. Tien Shan Geohazards Database: Landslide Susceptibility Analysis. *Geomorphology*. 249. pp. 32–43.

Figure 6: Landslide Susceptibility

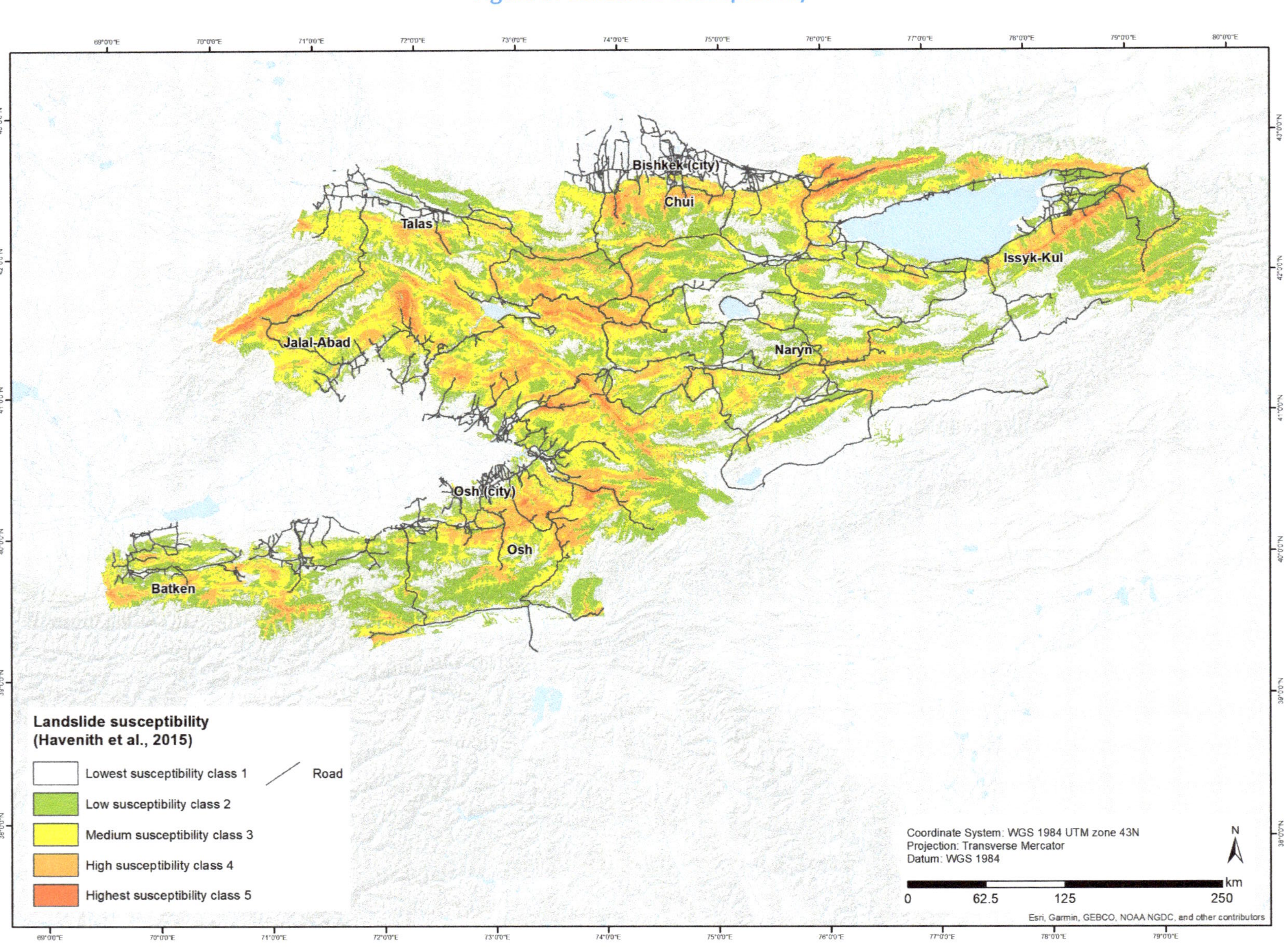

Sources: Basemap: Esri, Garmin, GEBCO, NOAA NGDC, other contributors; Roads: OpenStreetMap; Landslide susceptibility: H. Havenith et al. 2015. Tien Shan Geohazards Database: Landslide Susceptibility Analysis. *Geomorphology.* 249. pp. 32–43.

Figure 7: Factors Contributing to Landslide Susceptibility – Geology of the Kyrgyz Republic

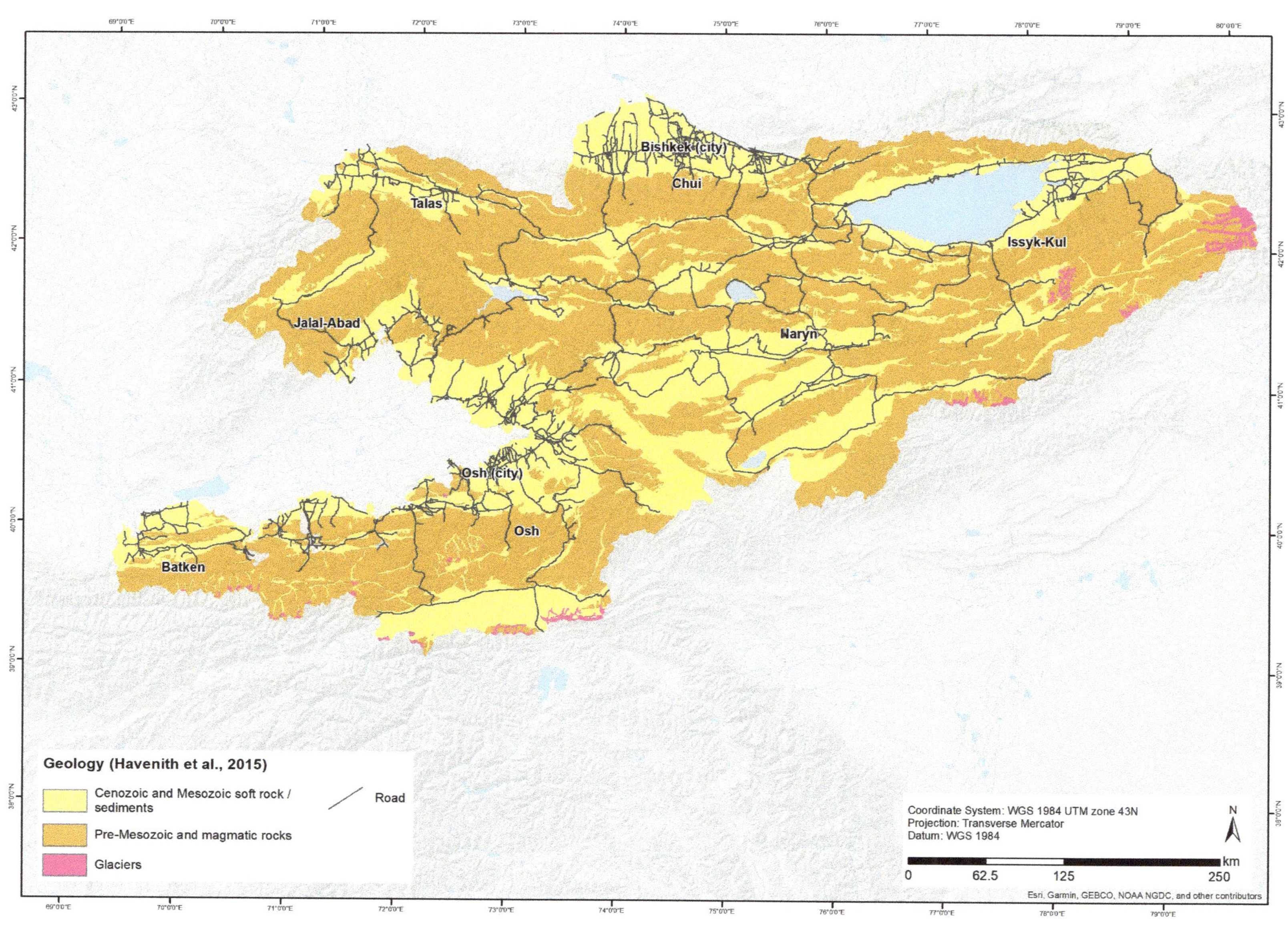

Sources: Basemap: Esri, Garmin, GEBCO, NOAA NGDC, other contributors; Roads: OpenStreetMap; Geology: H. Havenith et al. 2015. Tien Shan Geohazards Database: Landslide Susceptibility Analysis. *Geomorphology*. 249. pp. 32–43.

Figure 8: Factors Contributing to Landslide Susceptibility – Annual Average Precipitation in the Kyrgyz Republic

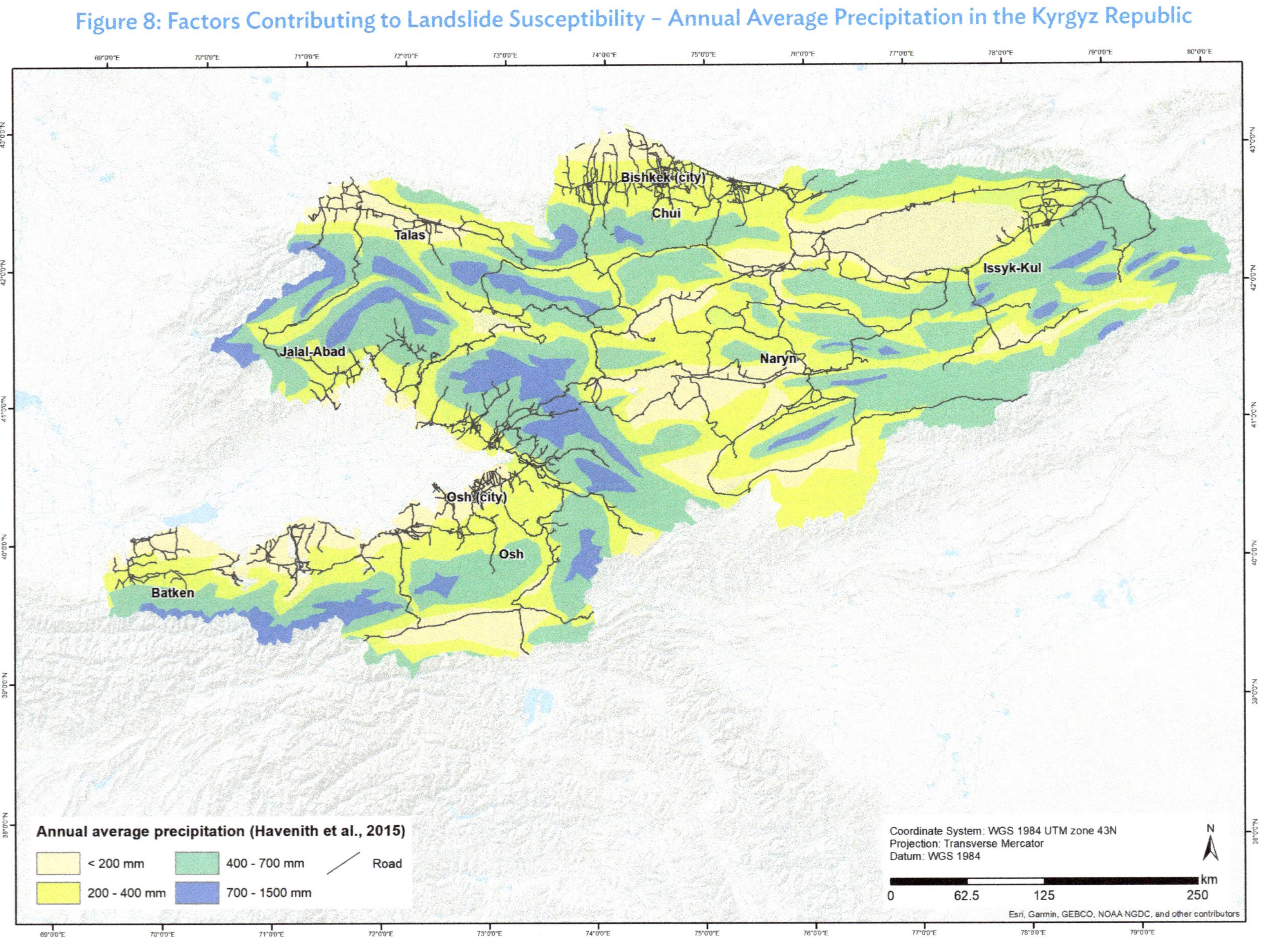

Sources: Basemap: Esri, Garmin, GEBCO, NOAA NGDC, other contributors; Roads: OpenStreetMap; Annual average precipitation: H. Havenith et al. 2015. Tien Shan Geohazards Database: Landslide Susceptibility Analysis. *Geomorphology*. 249. pp. 32–43.

Figure 9: Factors Contributing to Landslide Susceptibility – Active Faults and Peak Ground Acceleration

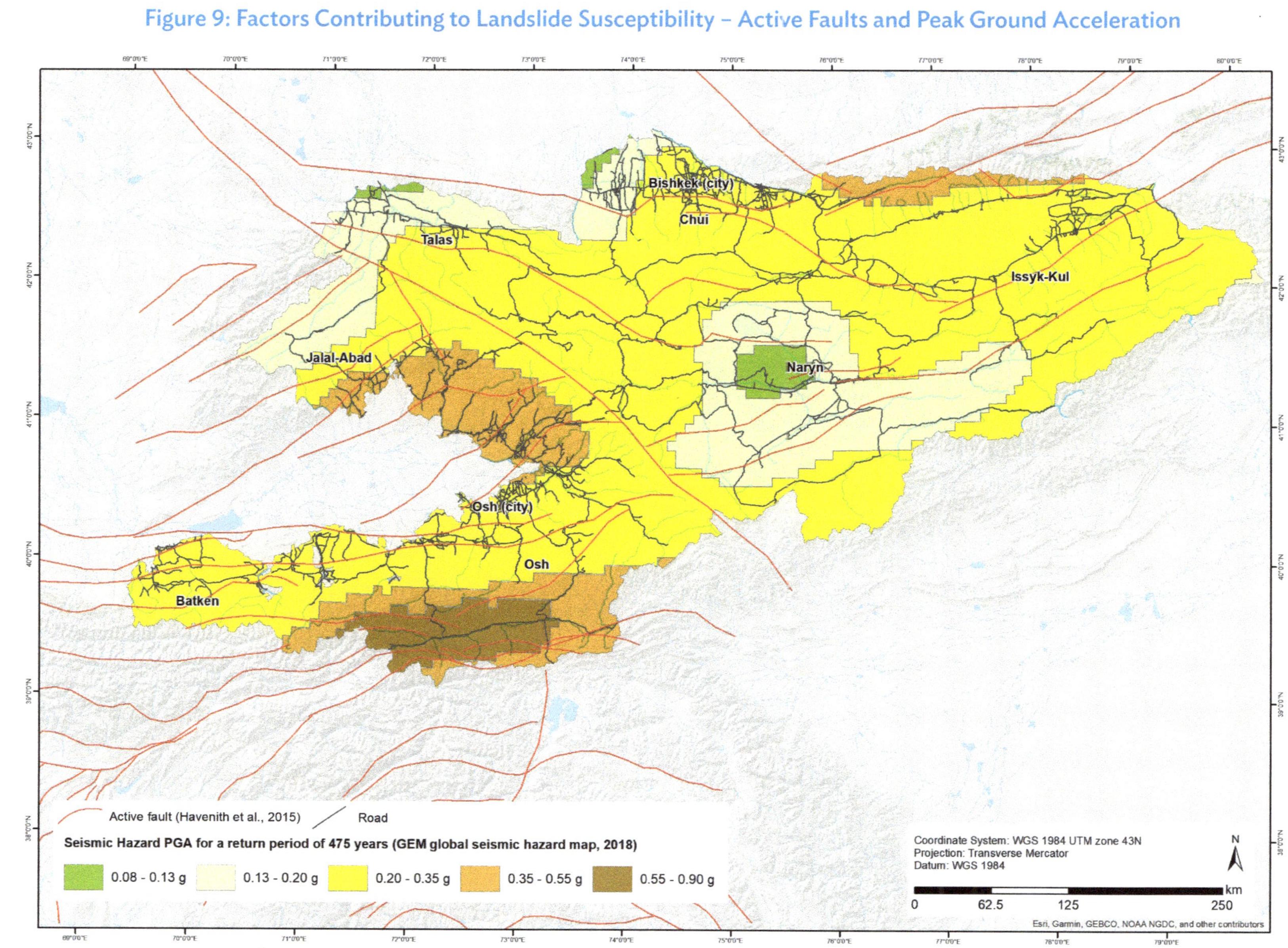

Sources: Basemap: Esri, Garmin, GEBCO, NOAA NGDC, other contributors; Roads: OpenStreetMap; Active faults: H. Havenith et al. 2015. Tien Shan Geohazards Database: Landslide Susceptibility Analysis. *Geomorphology*. 249. pp. 32–43; Seismic Hazard PGA: GEM. 2018. Global Earthquake Hazard Map.

Figure 10: Landslide Hazard Level

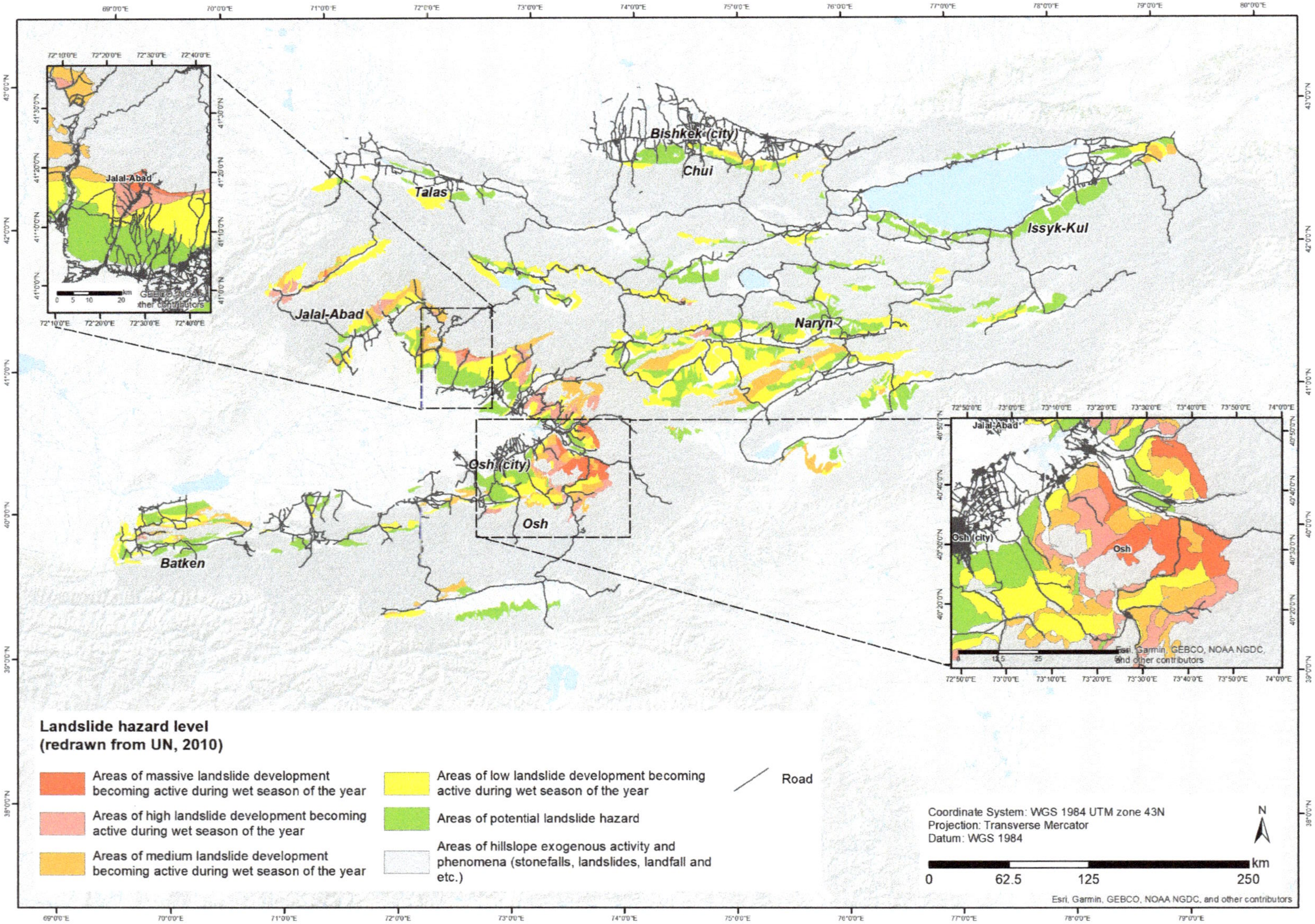

Sources: Basemap: Esri, Garmin, GEBCO, NOAA NGDC, other contributors; Roads: OpenStreetMap; Landslide hazard level: UNISDR. 2010. *In-depth Review of Disaster Risk Reduction in the Kyrgyz Republic.* Geneva.

Figure 11: Mudflow Hazard Level

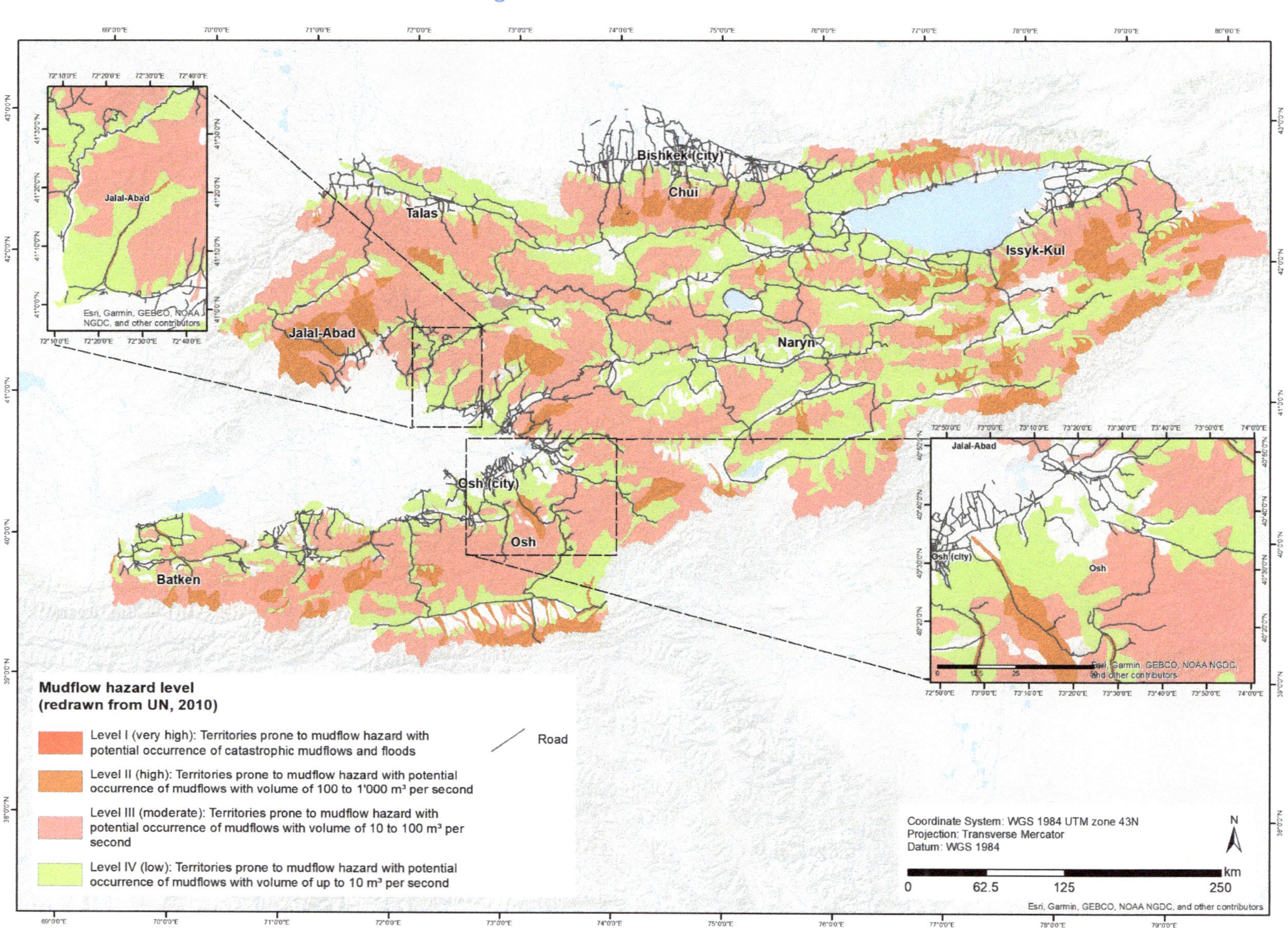

Sources: Basemap: Esri, Garmin, GEBCO, NOAA NGDC, other contributors; Roads: OpenStreetMap; Mudflow hazard level: UNISDR. 2010. *In-depth Review of Disaster Risk Reduction in the Kyrgyz Republic*. Geneva.

Figure 12: Landslide Susceptibility of Roads

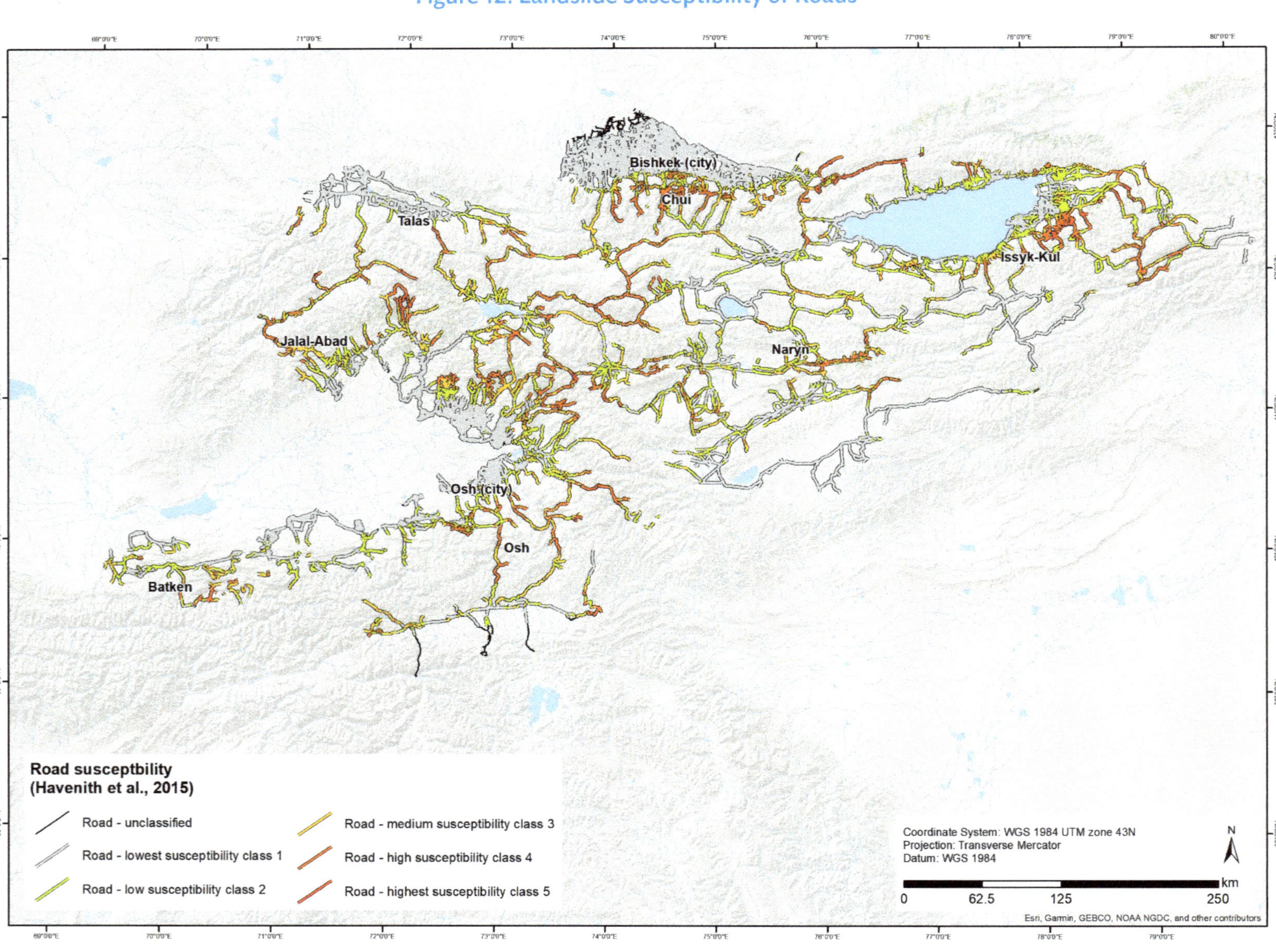

Sources: Basemap: Esri, Garmin, GEBCO, NOAA NGDC, and other contributors. Roads: OpenStreetmap. Susceptibility: H. Havenith et al. 2015. Tien Shan Geohazards Database: Landslide Susceptibility Analysis. *Geomorphology*. 249. pp. 32–43.

Figure 13: Landslide Susceptibility of Villages, Schools, and Hospitals

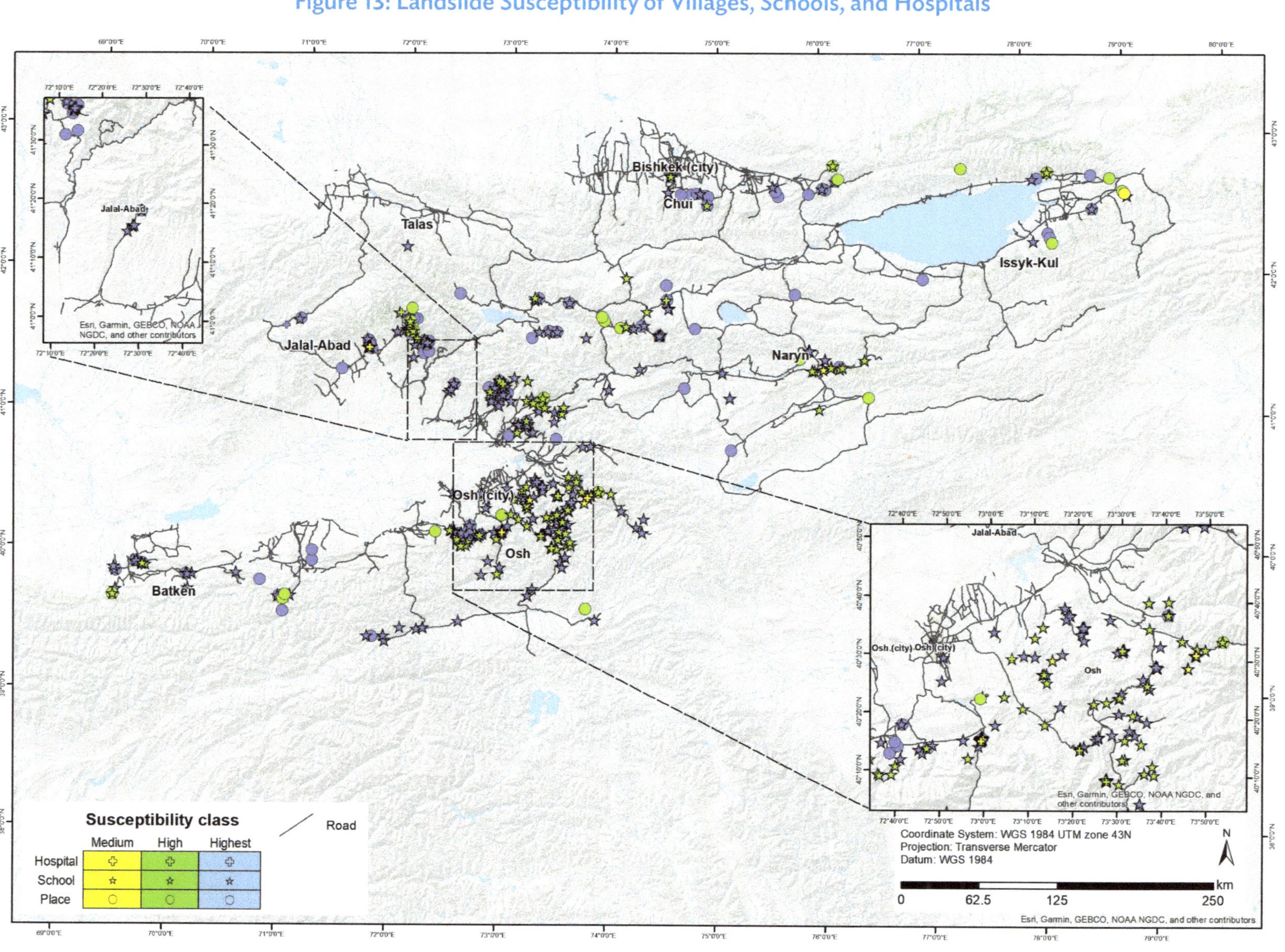

Sources: Basemap: Esri, Garmin, GEBCO, NOAA NGDC, and other contributors. Roads: OpenStreetmap. Susceptibility: H. Havenith et al. 2015. Tien Shan Geohazards Database: Landslide Susceptibility Analysis. *Geomorphology*. 249. pp. 32–43.

Figure 14: Location of 10 Case Studies in Landslide Modeling in Osh and Jalal-Abad Oblasts

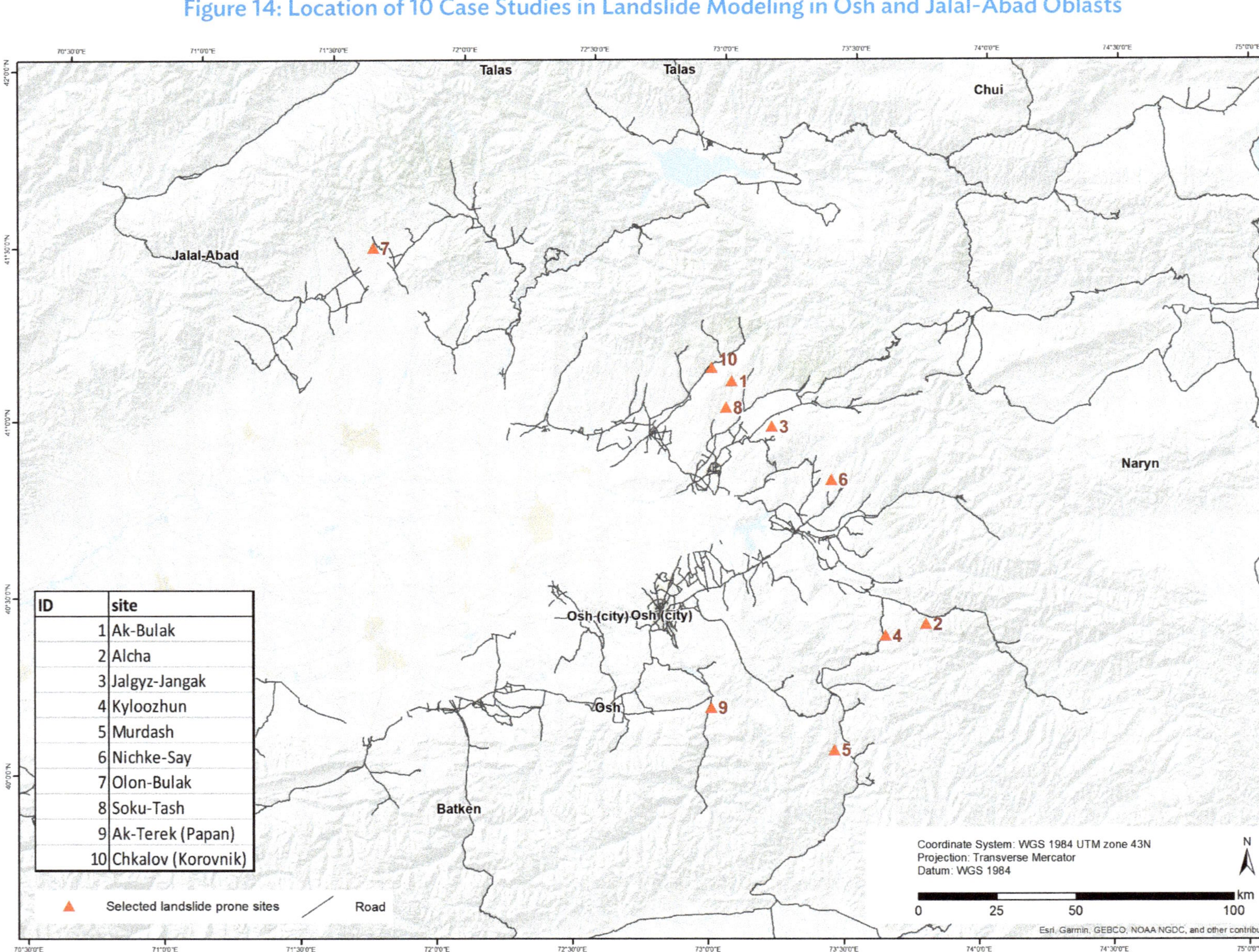

ID	site
1	Ak-Bulak
2	Alcha
3	Jalgyz-Jangak
4	Kyloozhun
5	Murdash
6	Nichke-Say
7	Olon-Bulak
8	Soku-Tash
9	Ak-Terek (Papan)
10	Chkalov (Korovnik)

Sources: Basemap: Esri, Garmin, GEBCO, NOAA NGDC, other contributors; Roads, rivers: OpenStreetMap; Selected landslide prone sites: Asian Development Bank. 2021. *Preparing the Landslide Risk Management Sector Project: Landslide Risk Assessment*. Consultant's Report. Manila.

Figure 15: Ak-Bulak Landslide, Suzak District – Geomorphological Lineaments and Modeled Spreading Area

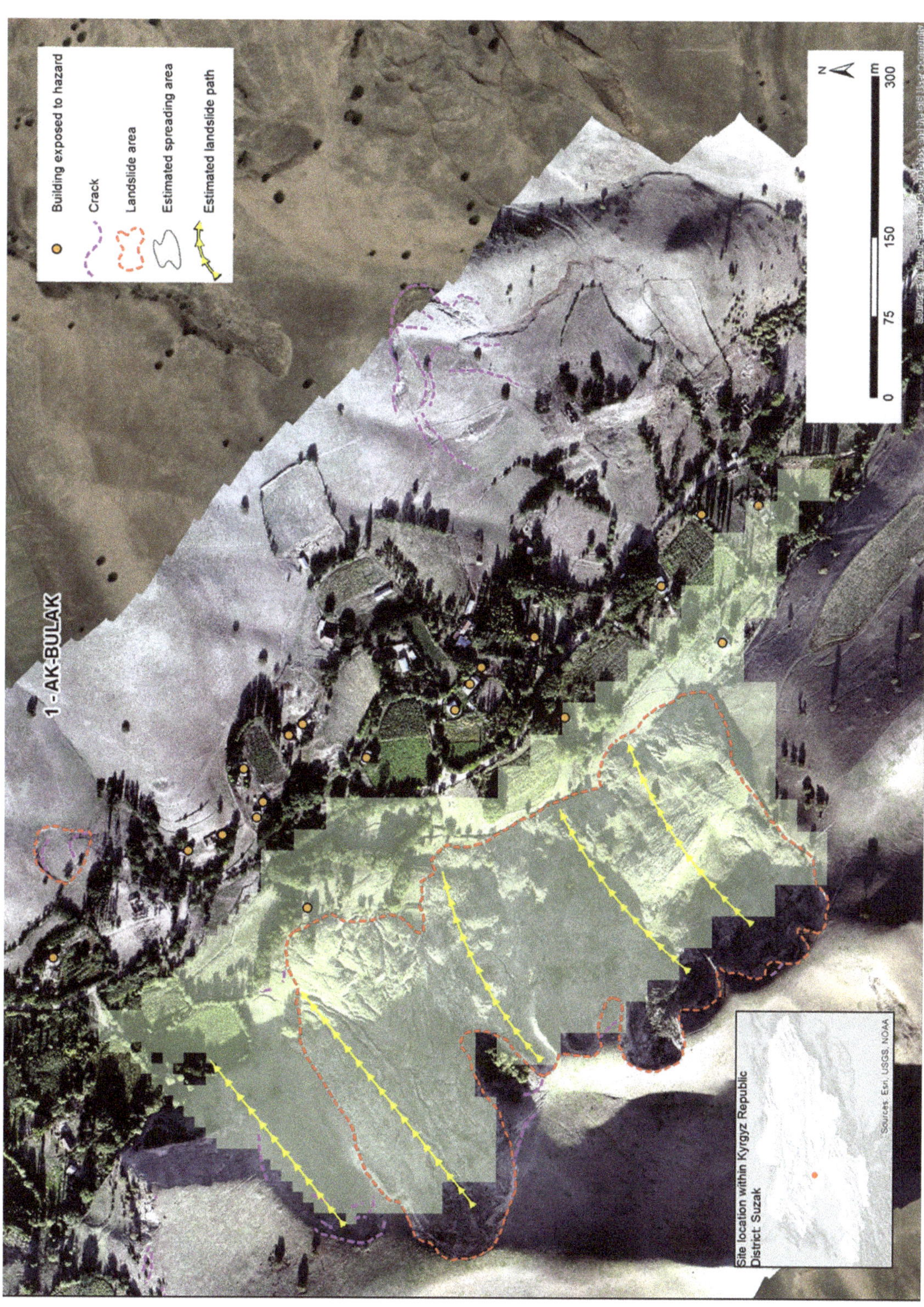

Sources: Basemap: Esir, Maxar, Earthstar Geographics, the GIS User Community; Drone imagery: CAIAG (2021); Buildings exposed to hazard, cracks, landslide area, estimated landslide path: Asian Development Bank. 2021. *Preparing the Landslide Risk Management Sector Project: Landslide Risk Assessment*. Consultant's Report. Manila; Hospitals exposed to hazard: MES field assessment (2020); Method for estimated spreading area: C. Huggel et al. 2003. Regional Scale GIS–Models for Assessment of Hazards from Glacier Lake Outbursts: Evaluation and Application in the Swiss Alps. *Natural Hazards and Earth System Sciences. 3.* pp. 647–662.

Figure 16: Alcha Landslide, Kara–Kulja District – Geomorphological Lineaments and Modeled Spreading Area

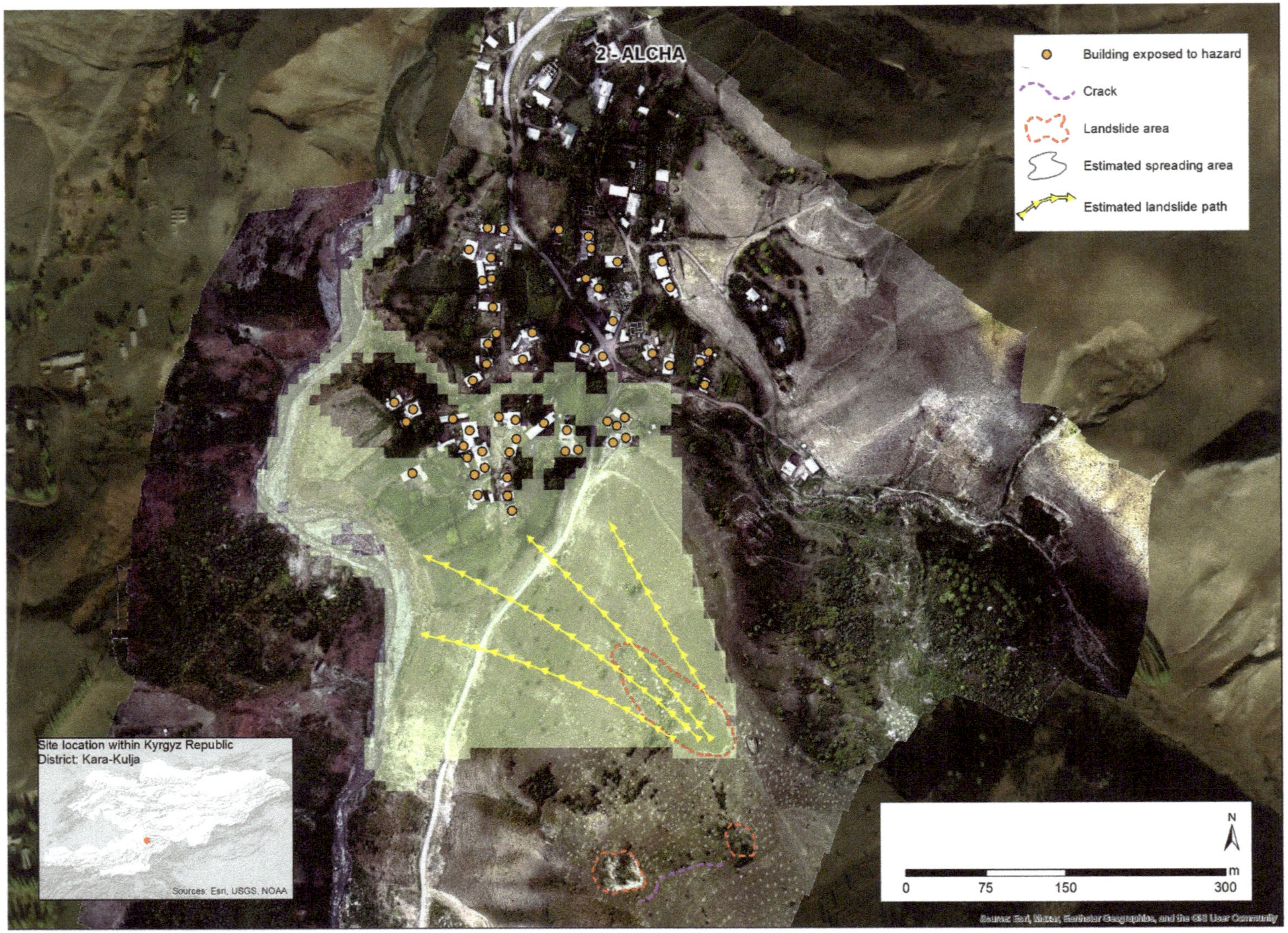

Sources: Basemap: Esir, Maxar, Earthstar Geographics, the GIS User Community; Drone imagery: CAIAG (2021); Buildings exposed to hazard, cracks, landslide area, estimated landslide path: Asian Development Bank. 2021. *Preparing the Landslide Risk Management Sector Project: Landslide Risk Assessment. Consultant's Report.* Manila; Hospitals exposed to hazard: MES field assessment (2020); Method for estimated spreading area: C. Huggel et al. 2003. Regional Scale GIS-Models for Assessment of Hazards from Glacier Lake Outbursts: Evaluation and Application in the Swiss Alps. *Natural Hazards and Earth System Sciences.* 3. pp. 647–662.

Figure 17: Jalgyz-Jangak Landslide, Suzak District – Geomorphological Lineaments and Modeled Spreading Area

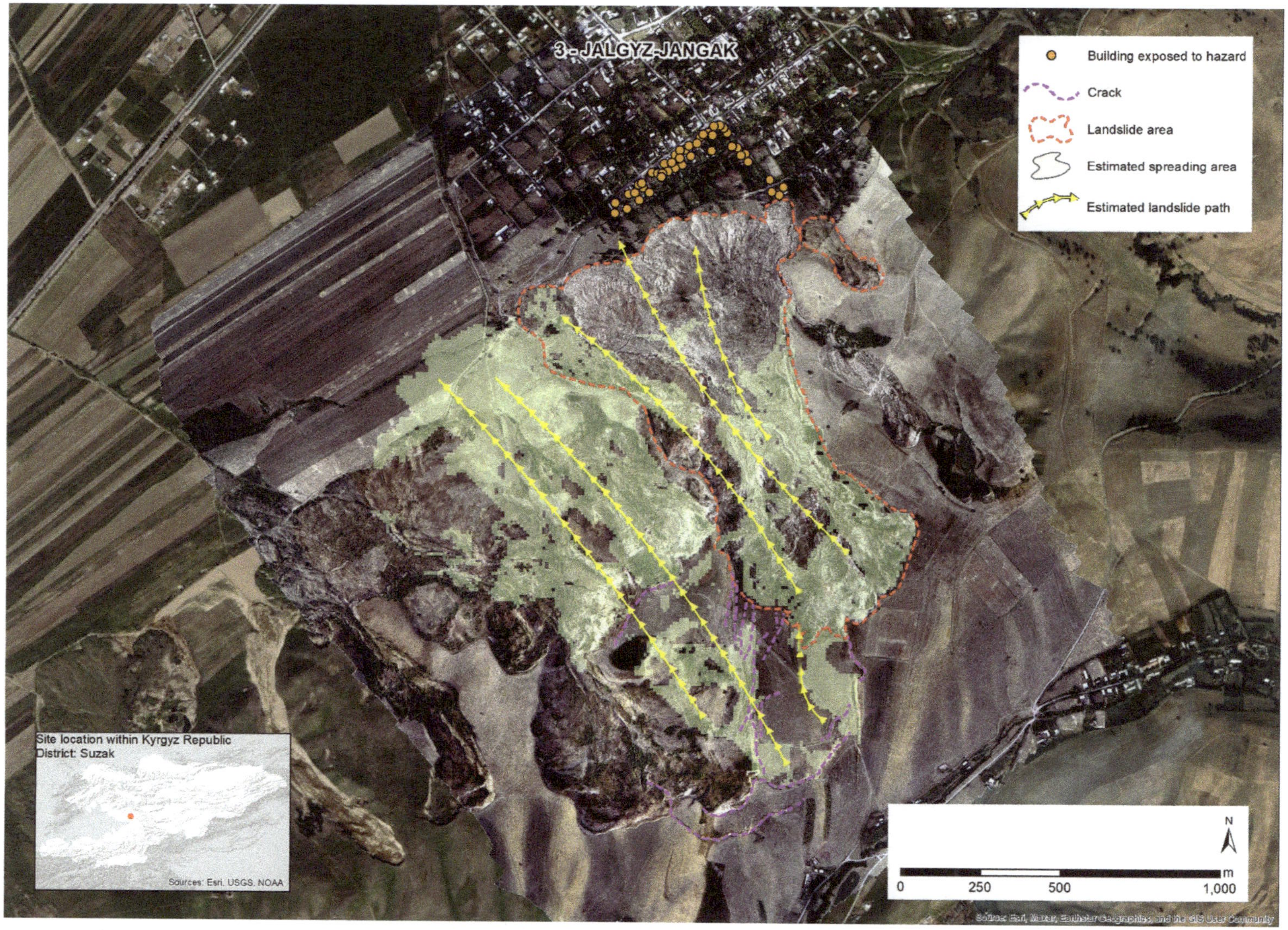

Sources: Basemap: Esir, Maxar, Earthstar Geographics, the GIS User Community; Drone imagery: CAIAG (2021); Buildings exposed to hazard, cracks, landslide area, estimated landslide path: Asian Development Bank. 2021. *Preparing the Landslide Risk Management Sector Project: Landslide Risk Assessment*. Consultant's Report. Manila; Hospitals exposed to hazard: MES field assessment (2020); Method for estimated spreading area: C. Huggel et al. 2003. Regional Scale GIS-Models for Assessment of Hazards from Glacier Lake Outbursts: Evaluation and Application in the Swiss Alps. *Natural Hazards and Earth System Sciences*. 3. pp. 647–662.

Sources: Basemap: Esri, Maxar, Earthstar Geographics, the GIS User Community; Drone imagery: CAIAG (2021); Buildings exposed to hazard, cracks, landslide area, estimated landslide path: Asian Development Bank. 2021. *Preparing the Landslide Risk Management Sector Project: Landslide Risk Assessment. Consultant's Report.* Manila; Hospitals exposed to hazard: MES field assessment (2020); Method for estimated spreading area: C. Huggel et al. 2003. Regional Scale GIS–Models for Assessment of Hazards from Glacier Lake Outbursts: Evaluation and Application in the Swiss Alps. *Natural Hazards and Earth System Sciences.* 3. pp. 647–662.

Figure 19: Murdash Landslide, Alai District – Geomorphological Lineaments and Modeled Spreading Area

Sources: Basemap: Esir, Maxar, Earthstar Geographics, the GIS User Community; Drone imagery: CAIAG (2021); Buildings exposed to hazard, cracks, landslide area, estimated landslide path: Asian Development Bank. 2021. *Preparing the Landslide Risk Management Sector Project: Landslide Risk Assessment*. Consultant's Report. Manila; Hospitals exposed to hazard: MES field assessment (2020); Method for estimated spreading area: C. Huggel et al. 2003. Regional Scale GIS-Models for Assessment of Hazards from Glacier Lake Outbursts: Evaluation and Application in the Swiss Alps. *Natural Hazards and Earth System Sciences*. 3. pp. 647–662.

Figure 20: Nichke–Say Landslide, Uzgen District – Geomorphological Lineaments and Modeled Spreading Area

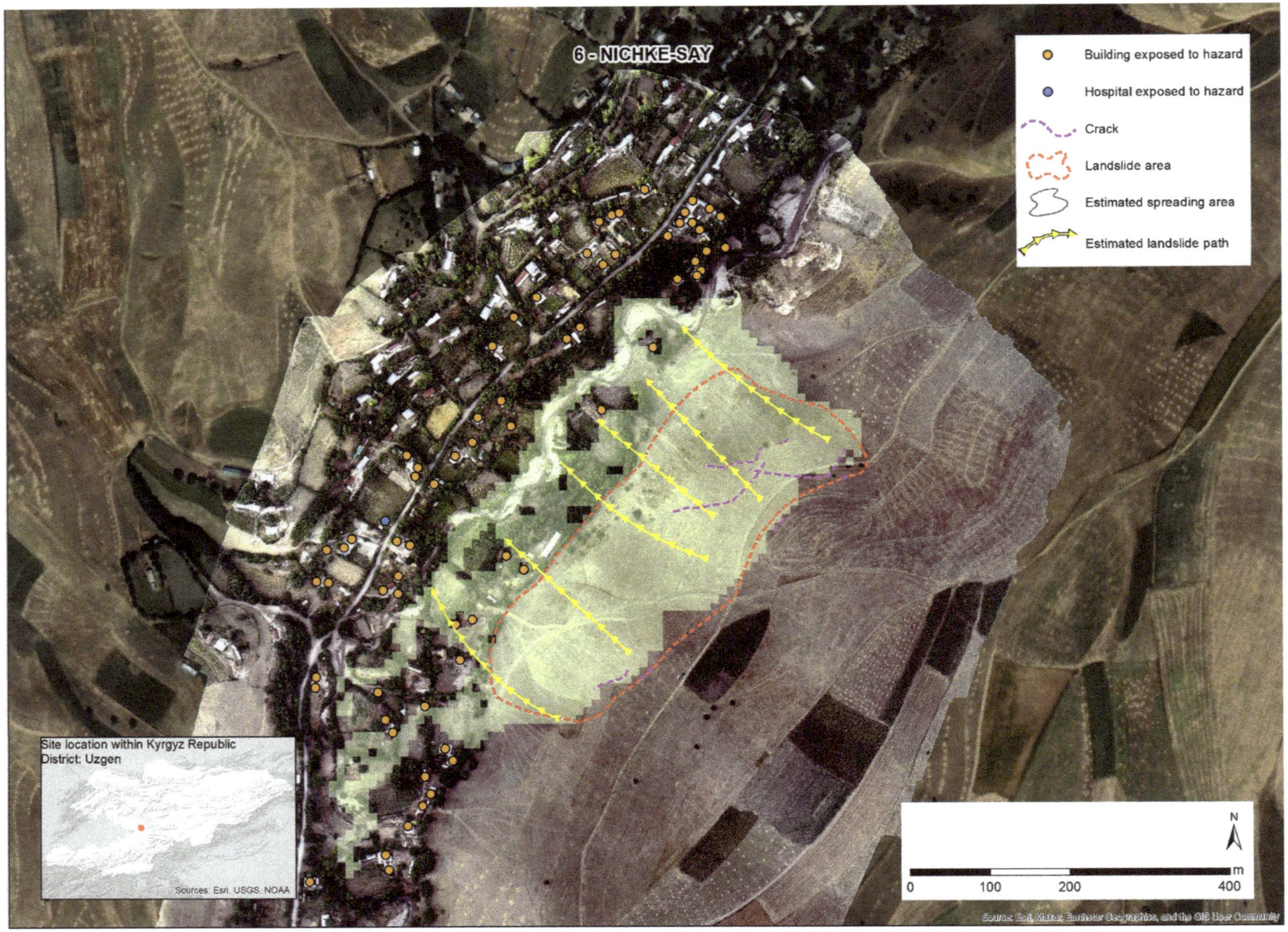

Sources: Basemap: Esri, Maxar, Earthstar Geographics, the GIS User Community; Drone imagery: CAIAG (2021); Buildings exposed to hazard, cracks, landslide area, estimated landslide path: Asian Development Bank. 2021. *Preparing the Landslide Risk Management Sector Project: Landslide Risk Assessment.* Consultant's Report. Manila; Hospitals exposed to hazard: MES field assessment (2020); Method for estimated spreading area: C. Huggel et al. 2003. Regional Scale GIS-Models for Assessment of Hazards from Glacier Lake Outbursts: Evaluation and Application in the Swiss Alps. *Natural Hazards and Earth System Sciences. 3.* pp. 647–662.

Figure 21: Olon–Bulak Landslide, Aksy District – Geomorphological Lineaments and Modeled Spreading Area

Sources: Basemap: Esir, Maxar, Earthstar Geographics, the GIS User Community; Drone imagery: CAIAG (2021); Buildings exposed to hazard, cracks, landslide area, estimated landslide path: Asian Development Bank. 2021. *Preparing the Landslide Risk Management Sector Project: Landslide Risk Assessment. Consultant's Report*. Manila; Hospitals exposed to hazard: MES field assessment (2020); Method for estimated spreading area: C. Huggel et al. 2003. Regional Scale GIS-Models for Assessment of Hazards from Glacier Lake Outbursts: Evaluation and Application in the Swiss Alps. *Natural Hazards and Earth System Sciences.* 3. pp. 647–662.

Figure 22: Soku–Tash Landslide, Suzak District – Geomorphological Lineaments and Modeled Spreading Area

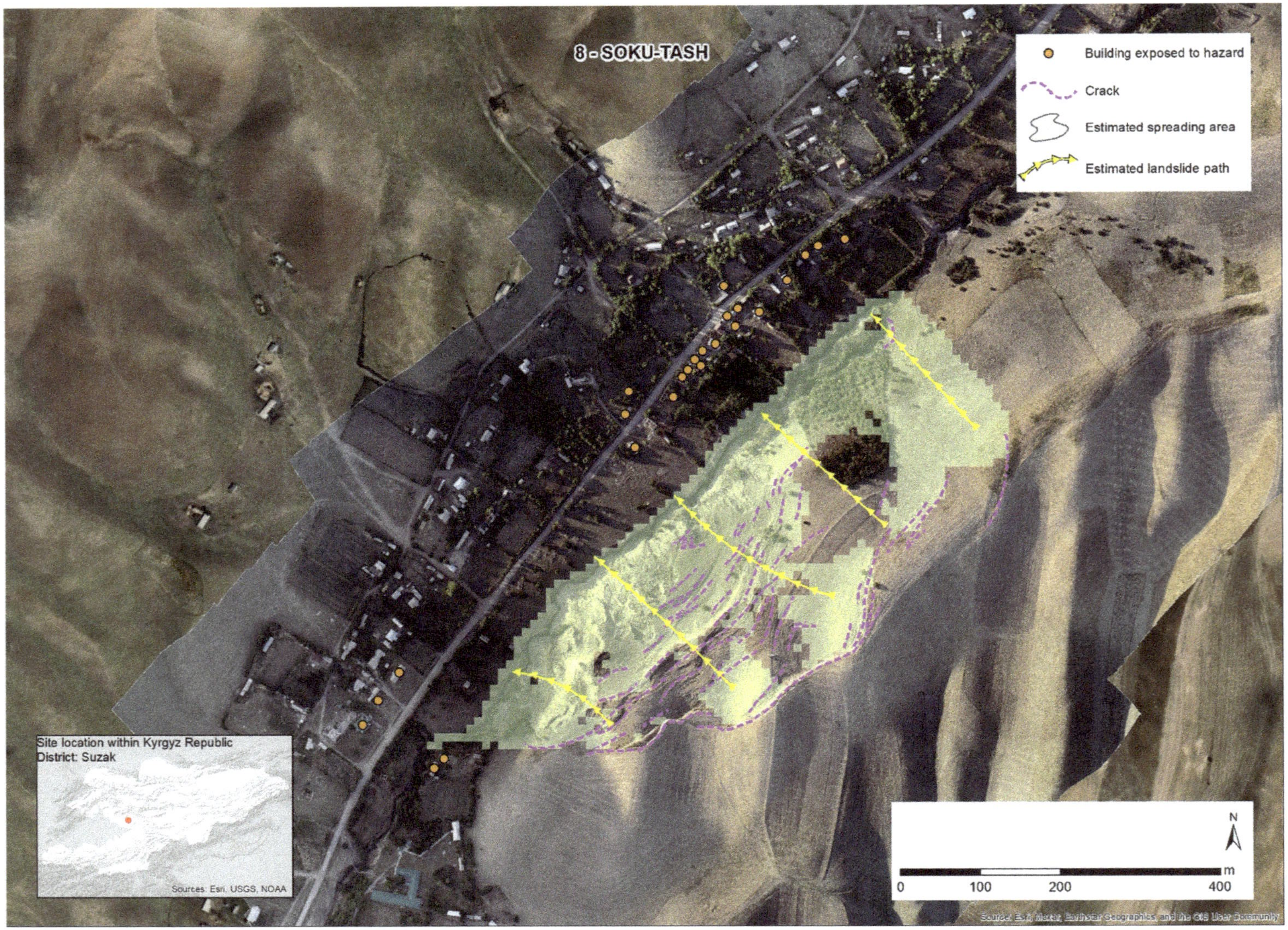

Sources: Basemap: Esri, Maxar, Earthstar Geographics, the GIS User Community; Drone imagery: CAIAG (2021); Buildings exposed to hazard, cracks, landslide area, estimated landslide path: Asian Development Bank. 2021. *Preparing the Landslide Risk Management Sector Project: Landslide Risk Assessment.* Consultant's Report. Manila; Hospitals exposed to hazard: MES field assessment (2020); Method for estimated spreading area: C. Huggel et al. 2003. Regional Scale GIS–Models for Assessment of Hazards from Glacier Lake Outbursts: Evaluation and Application in the Swiss Alps. *Natural Hazards and Earth System Sciences.* 3. pp. 647–662.

Figure 23: Ak-Terek (Papan) Landslide, Kara-Suu District – Geomorphological Lineaments and Modeled Spreading Area

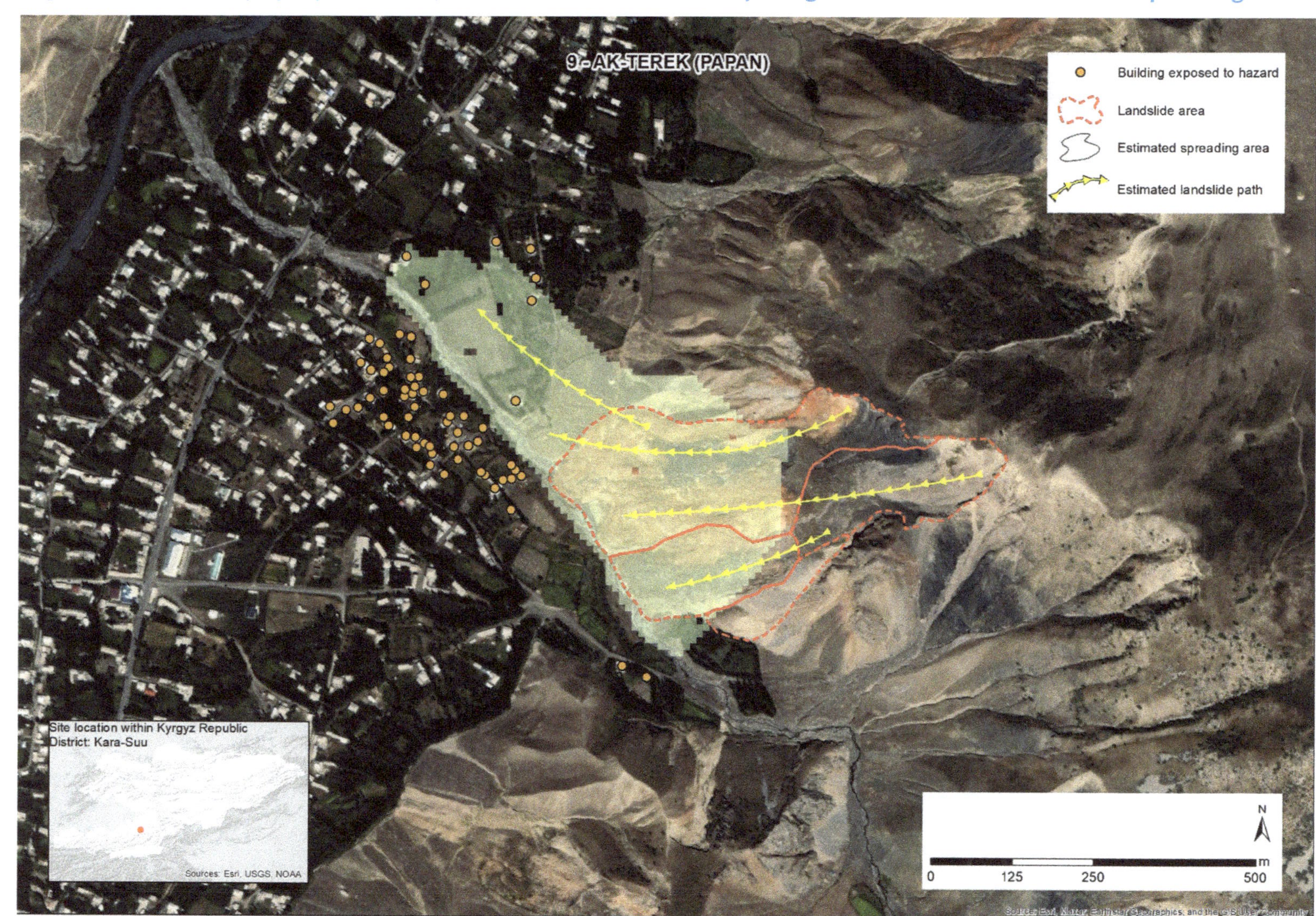

Sources: Basemap: Esir, Maxar, Earthstar Geographics, the GIS User Community; Drone imagery: CAIAG (2021); Buildings exposed to hazard, cracks, landslide area, estimated landslide path: Asian Development Bank. 2021. *Preparing the Landslide Risk Management Sector Project: Landslide Risk Assessment*. Consultant's Report. Manila; Hospitals exposed to hazard: MES field assessment (2020); Method for estimated spreading area: C. Huggel et al. 2003. Regional Scale GIS-Models for Assessment of Hazards from Glacier Lake Outbursts: Evaluation and Application in the Swiss Alps. *Natural Hazards and Earth System Sciences*. 3. pp. 647–662.

Figure 24: Chkalov Landslide, Bazar-Korgon District – Geomorphological Lineaments and Modeled Spreading Area

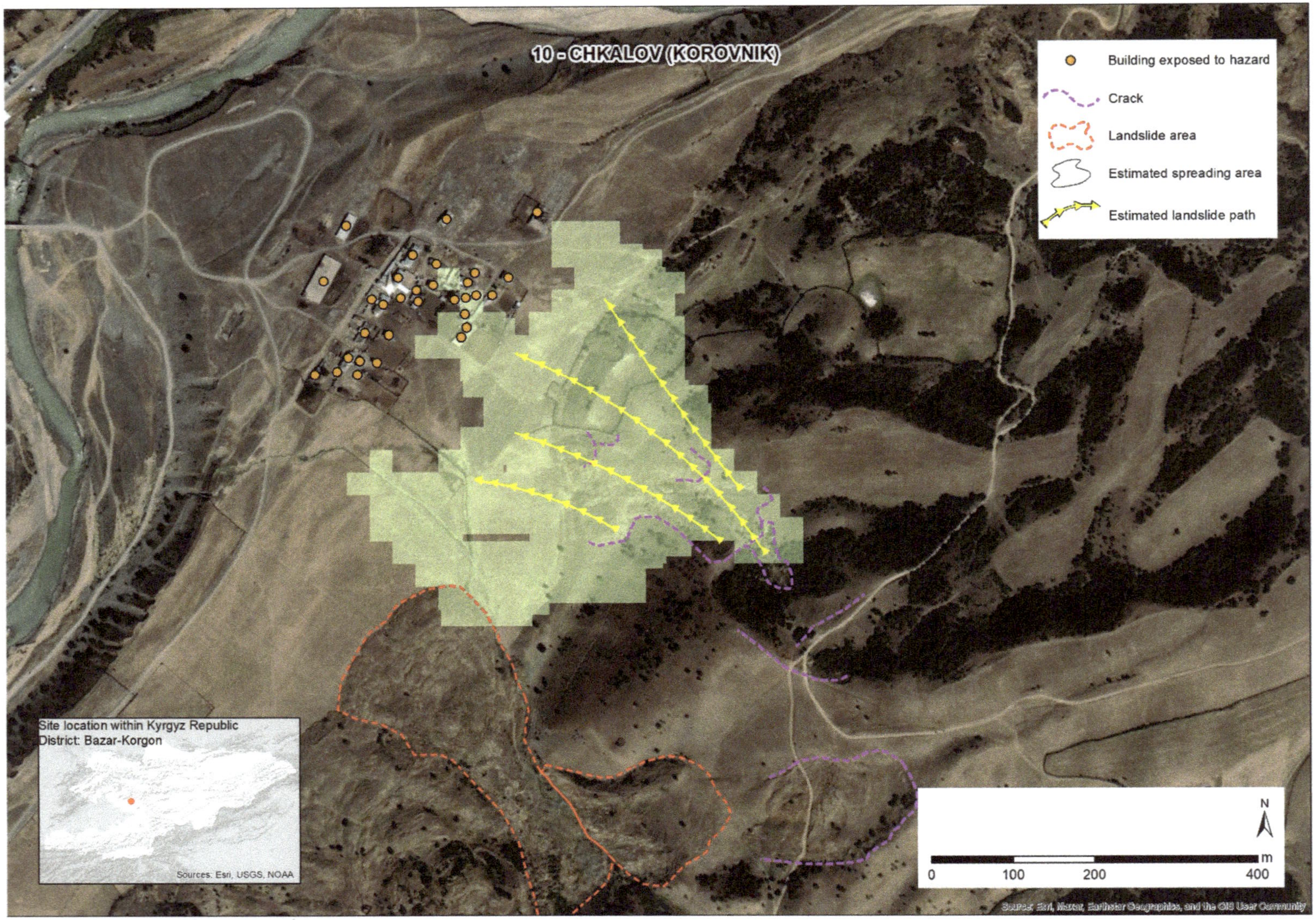

Sources: Basemap: Esri, Maxar, Earthstar Geographics, the GIS User Community; Drone imagery: CAIAG (2021); Buildings exposed to hazard, cracks, landslide area, estimated landslide path: Asian Development Bank. 2021. *Preparing the Landslide Risk Management Sector Project: Landslide Risk Assessment. Consultant's Report*. Manila; Hospitals exposed to hazard: MES field assessment (2020); Method for estimated spreading area: C. Huggel et al. 2003. Regional Scale GIS-Models for Assessment of Hazards from Glacier Lake Outbursts: Evaluation and Application in the Swiss Alps. *Natural Hazards and Earth System Sciences*. 3. pp. 647–662.

5. Ayusai: A Case Study on Integrated Landslide Risk Management

In the early morning on 29 April 2017, a devastating landslide struck Ayusai, in the west of Ayu village, Uzgen district, Osh oblast. The landslide killed 24 people and destroyed several houses and the only road connecting Ayusai to the rest of the village. It was the deadliest landslide in the region in 15 years.

The government responded quickly, providing food and temporary housing and shelter and rebuilding the road network and community infrastructure. A resettlement program was started to move at-risk families to safer locations. But some relocated families soon returned to Ayusai, because of the ties within their ethnic Turkish community, going back to their familiar productive grazing and irrigated land.

Six years later, the people and livelihoods of Ayusai are still at risk of landslides from multiple unstable zones along the slopes lining this part of the village. Landslide risk management remains an ongoing priority for the people and the government. ADB is supporting the reduction and management of landslide risks in Ayusai through the *Landslide Risk Management Sector Project*.[75]

Landslide of 2017, Ayusai village, Osh oblast. The village was selected for priority investment under the ADB Landslide Risk Management Sector Project (photo by International Centre for Environmental Management).

---

[75] ADB. Kyrgyz Republic: Landslide Risk Management Sector Project.

Key Figures about Ayu Village

- Population: 1,302 people, of whom 615 are male (47%) and 687 female (53%) – with the overall population increasing over the past 10 years.

- Infrastructure: Ayu has a total of 220 houses. The village has 8 kilometer (km) of rural roads. Every household is connected to the main village road, which is unpaved and of low quality. The village has one high school. There is a primary school 5 km from the village. The village has power transmission lines and a cellphone network. All households are connected to the national electrical power grid. There is no drinking water supply or wastewater disposal system. All households collect water for domestic use from springs, which flow all year round. Pit latrines provide sanitation.

- Economy: Ayu is a rural settlement where the main occupation is farming, mainly crop cultivation, home gardens, and livestock (cattle, horses, poultry). The large majority of farmland is rain-fed. The main sources of water for irrigation are the river and springs. On average, remittances contribute 40% of household income.

- Social development: The poverty rate in Ayu village stands at 10% of all households. Food insecurity is moderate and the malnutrition rate is approximately 30% of all households.

Source: Source: Ministry of Emergency Situations. 2021. Land Acquisition and Resettlement Plan: Ayusai Representative Subproject. Prepared for ADB under Kyrgyz Republic: Landslide Risk Management Sector Project.

Landslide Site Characteristics

A landslide risk assessment of the Ayusai site was carried out in 2020, with ADB technical assistance, integrating analysis of hazard, exposure, and vulnerability (footnote 15). The Ayusai landslide site lies in the western part of the village, in the valley of the Ayusai stream, a right tributary to the Zerger River. It is at an elevation of 1,350–1,500 masl. The area is characterized by small watersheds, rounded hills, some relict terraces, and many traces of past landslides. The climate is continental, with moderately cold winters, warm summers, and low rainfall. The average yearly rainfall is 587 mm, peaking in April–May, with a secondary, less significant, peak in October–November. Maximum daily precipitation is 40 mm. Slope instability in the area owes to the presence of water at the interface between the loess and the rock sub-base below and a fully saturated slope, during heavy prolonged rains or snow melting.

The entire Ayusai landslide slope has three identified landslide areas (Figure 25):

- The landslide that occurred in 2017;

- An 80-year-old landslide reportedly partially reactivated in 2016;

- The "village landslide": an unstable landslide area immediately above the secondary school under construction (no. 4 on the figure), where signs of distress are already visible.

The risk assessment was carried out based on a runout analysis aimed at defining the potential landslide spreading area and utilizing data from detailed physical asset surveys and satellite and drone imagery. Based on the risk assessment results (Figure 26), 1 house has been classified as located in a high-risk area, 10 buildings – including 1 school under construction – as in a moderate-risk area, and 59 buildings and rural infrastructure as in a low-risk area.

Figure 25: The Main Three Landslide Occurrences in the Ayusai Area

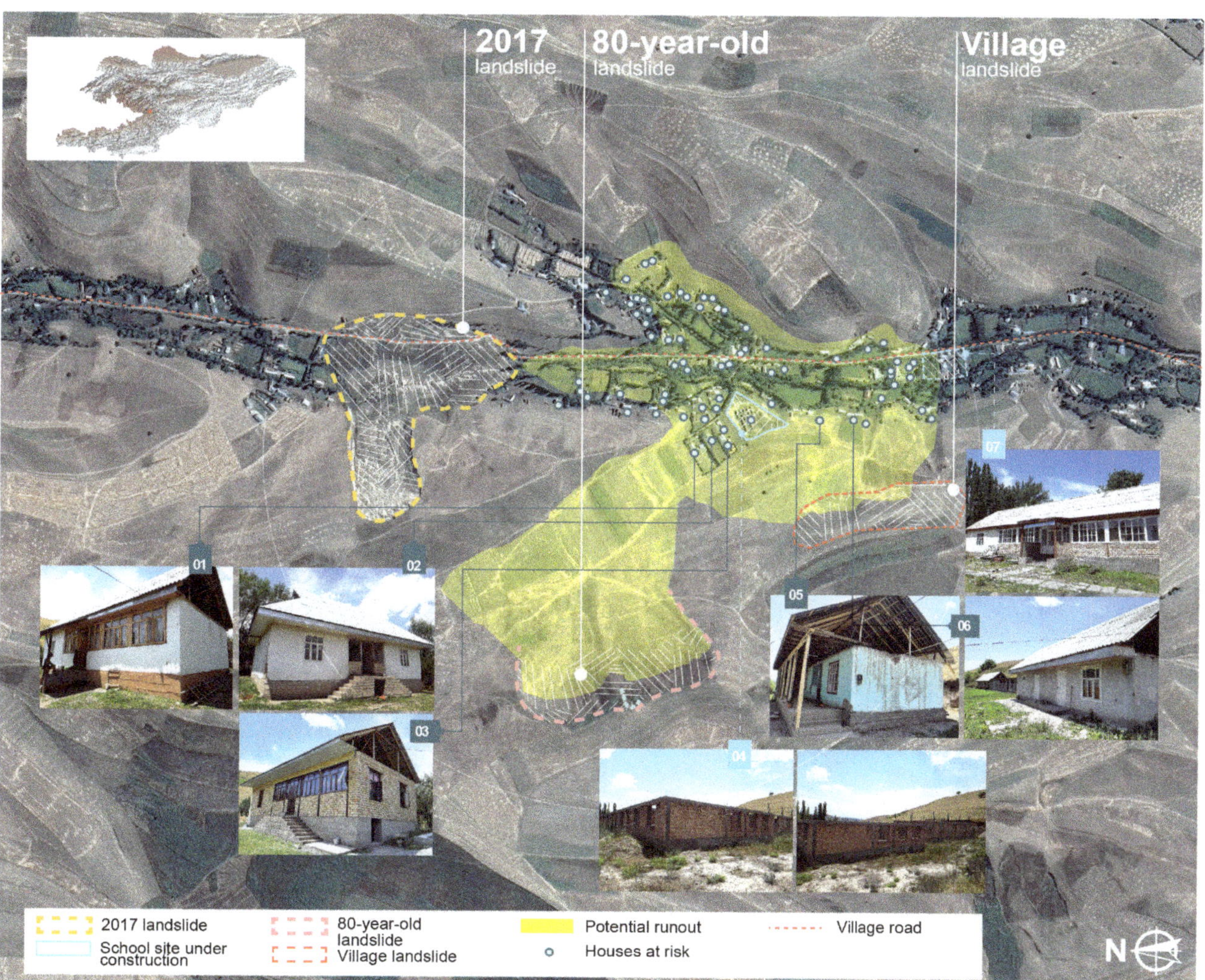

Sources: Developed by International Centre for Environmental Management, based on information from Asian Development Bank. 2021. *Preparing the Landslide Risk Management Sector Project: Landslide Risk Assessment.* Consultant's Report. Manila.

Figure 26: Landslide Risk Map of the Ayusai Landslide Site (top) and the Location of Ayusai within the Larger Ayu Village (bottom)

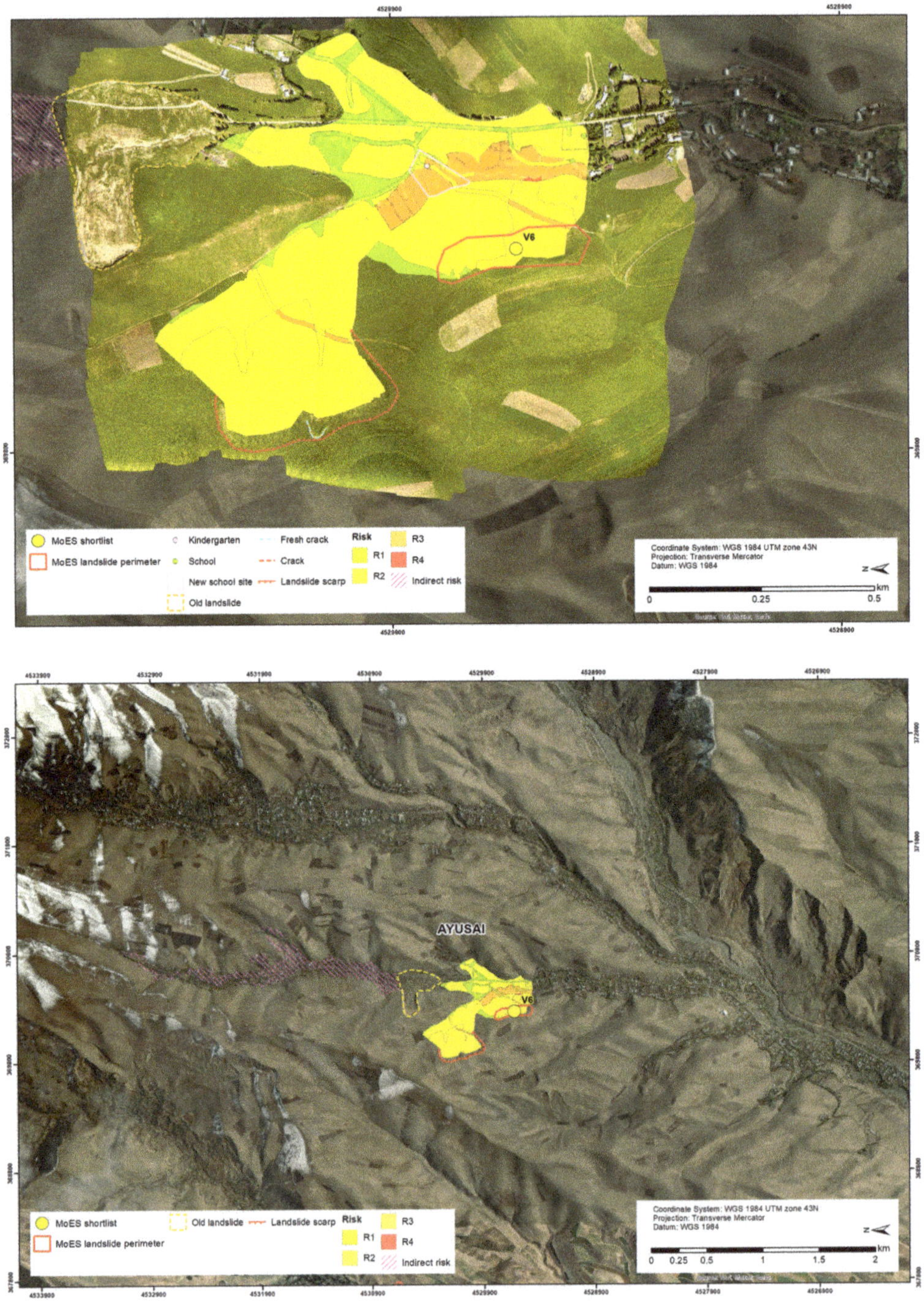

Note: The risk classes are defined as follows: very high (R4), high (R3), moderate (R2), and low (R2). The "indirect risk" class represents the part of Ayusai (north of the 2017 landslide) where temporary impacts or "damages" are expected in case of a landslide collapse blocking the only road to this area, resulting in a lack of access and possible interruption to services.

Sources: Basemap: Esir, Maxar, Earthstar Geographics, the GIS User Community; Drone imagery, new school site, old landslides, fresh cracks, landslide scarp: Asian Development Bank. 2021. *Preparing the Landslide Risk Management Sector Project: Technical Feasibility Study – Ayusai Subproject*. Consultant's Report. Manila; Schools, kindergartens, Ministry of Education and Science (MoES) shortlist, MoES landslide perimieter: Ministry of Emergency Situations field assessment (2020).

Community Awareness

Community awareness on where and why landslides are happening and what can be done about them is an essential foundation for effective landslide risk management.

A large majority of people in Ayusai hoped they would not be affected. In addition, people lacked sufficient information about the risk and/or saw the risk of staying as lower than the risk of relocating. People also hoped the government would protect people and prevent the landslide from happening; otherwise they did not know what to do.

People in Ayu had a good knowledge of landslide risk in the village and what to do about it, especially since the most recent landslide event in 2017 (Figure 27). However, there were notable gender differences, with awareness higher among men than women.

A total of 79% of people said there were rules that people living in or near landslide-prone areas should abide by. Again, there was a considerable gender difference, with more men (92%) than women (49%) stating awareness of such rules. Half of the people believed these rules were followed and the other half did not.

The most commonly mentioned rules were:

- Do not graze cattle on dangerous slopes.
- Do not live in or near a landslide-prone area.
- Do not irrigate farmland on or near a landslide-prone slope.

Focus group discussions with at-risk community, Ayusai village, Osh oblast. The feasibility study for the Ayusai subproject under the ADB Landslide Risk Management Sector Project included detailed consultations for the design of priority interventions (photo by International Centre for Environmental Management).

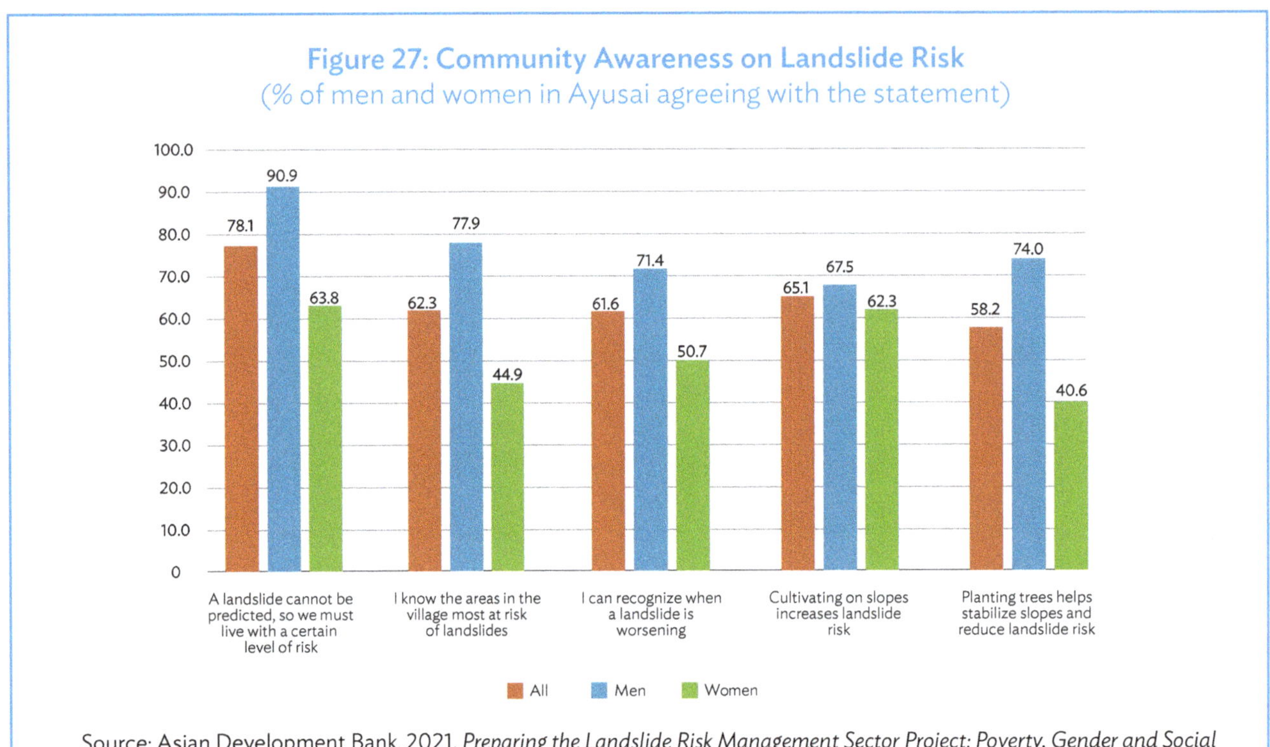

Source: Asian Development Bank. 2021. *Preparing the Landslide Risk Management Sector Project: Poverty, Gender and Social Assessment.* Consultant's Report. *Manila.*

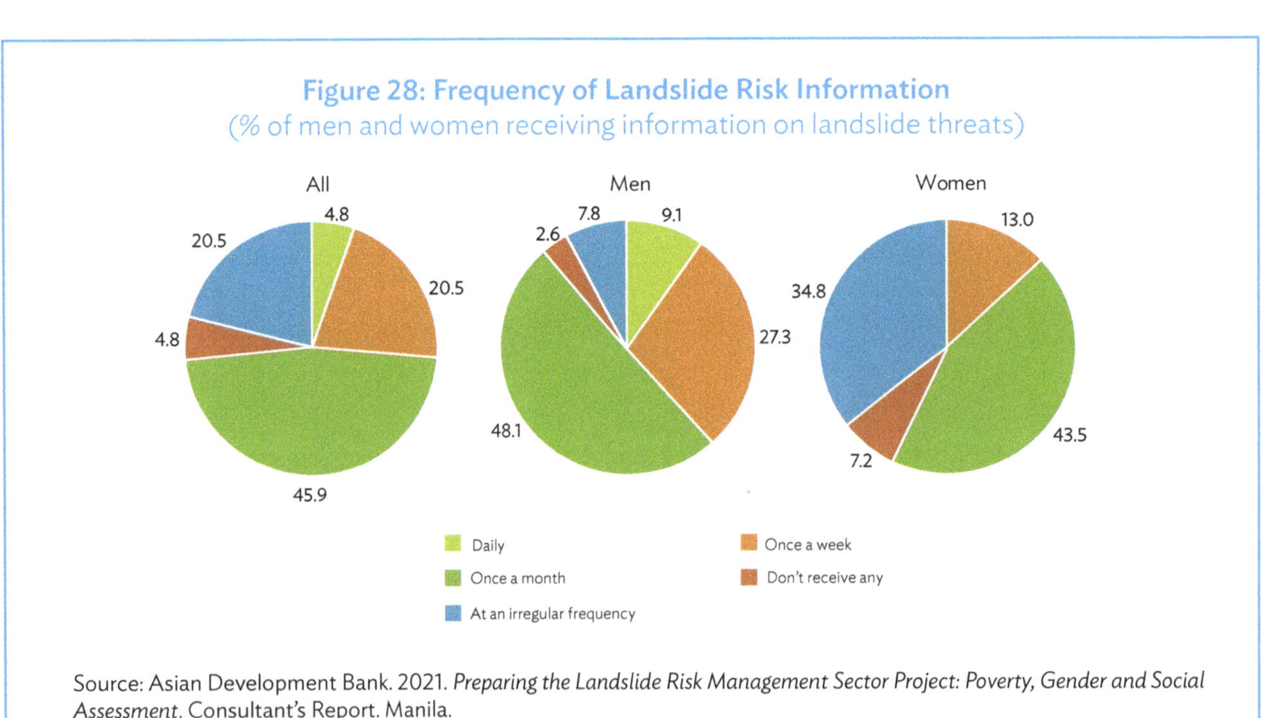

Source: Asian Development Bank. 2021. *Preparing the Landslide Risk Management Sector Project: Poverty, Gender and Social Assessment.* Consultant's Report. Manila.

- Do not walk on or go close to the landslide-prone slope.

- Do not cultivate anything on the landslide-prone slope.

- Children cannot play near a landslide-prone area.

- Do not construct any houses or structures on the landslide-prone slope.

- If there are changes in the springs, immediately inform the relevant local authorities.

In general, most people in Ayusai receive information on landslide threats regularly, although women do so more irregularly than men (Figure 28). However, a majority of people stated that the landslide risk and early warning information received was sometimes late, incomplete, unclear, and not useful. A total of 63% of people wanted more information on landslide risk (55% of men and 73% of women).

Solutions for Landslide Risk Management

Addressing landslide risk in Ayusai – and similar landslide-prone areas – requires an integrated package of interventions.

Soil sampling of Ayusai slope, Osh oblast. The feasibility study for the Ayusai subproject under the ADB Landslide Risk Management Sector Project included detailed site investigations to assess the soil characteristics of the target landslides (photo by International Centre for Environmental Management).

The following measures are proposed for implementation in the ADB-supported Landslide Risk Management Sector Project.

Physical measures:

- Unloading of slope areas where the loess layer is thicker, by excavating the material in excess and transferring it to soil disposal sites (Figure 29);

- Reshaping of other areas on the slope where bulging, opening cracks, etc. suggest potential future slope instability;

- Surface water drainage, via ditch collection on the slope;

- Spring catchment and collection in the limited areas where there are water springs or where the ground appears to be wet;

- Revegetation of the entire excavated area by sowing local grass and shrubs to restore the original landscape and allow crop cultivation and grazing for the local people;

- Disposal of excavated soil on designated safe sites, for example the 2007 landslide runout area;

- Rehabilitation of disposal sites as reclaimed agricultural or recreational land (Figure 29).

Nonstructural measures:

- Installation of on-site landslide monitoring and an early warning system for operation during the execution of the works and at the disposal sites, with potential community involvement in operation and maintenance of the monitoring system;

- Peer-to-peer learning and exchange visits of Ayusai community representatives to other landslide sites where landslide risk mitigation measures will be implemented;

- Training for community representatives and local authorities on gender differences in landslide risk, women's empowerment, and gender equality in disaster risk management.

Figure 29: Planned Designs for Unloading of the Landslide Slope Areas in Ayusai

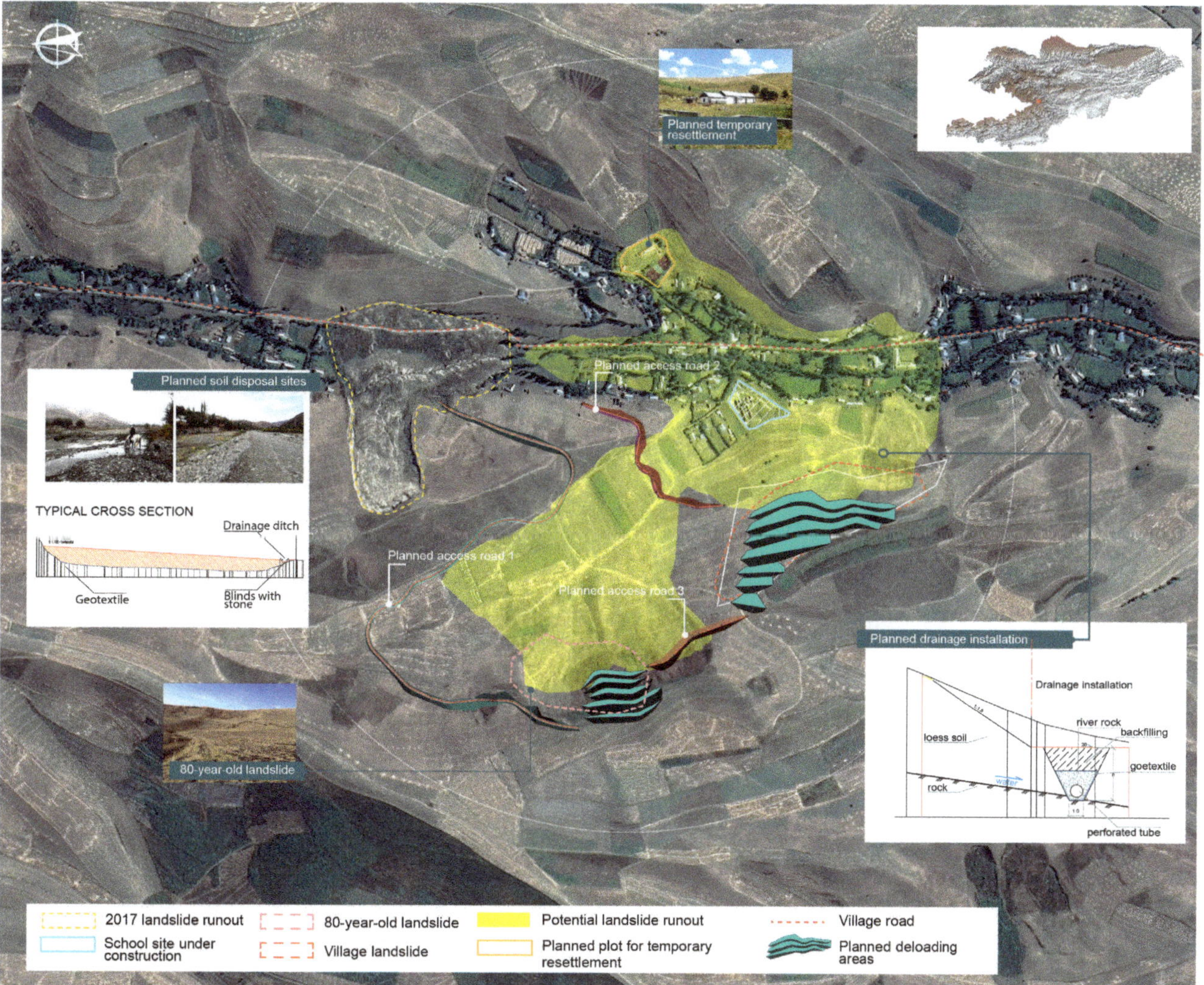

Source: Designed by International Centre for Environmental Management, utilizing information from Asian Development Bank. 2021. *Preparing the Landslide Risk Management Sector Project: Concept Design for Landslide Risk Mitigation Measures in the Ayusai Representative Subproject. Consultant's Report. Manila.*

6. Priorities and Way Forward

Landslides pose a significant and growing risk to the Kyrgyz Republic. The threat of landslides is part of daily life for many communities in rural parts of the Kyrgyz Republic. Out of over 4,500 landslides identified in the country, about 1,200 are considered active and threatening rural settlements and critical facilities such as roads, energy infrastructure, hospitals, and schools. About 30,000 people are considered to be at risk.

The Government of the Kyrgyz Republic has made landslide risk management a key priority. With support from various development partners, it has invested a great deal in monitoring, forecasting, early warning, small-scale risk mitigation measures, regreening, resettlement, and education and awareness-raising. There remains scope for improvement, however.

Proactive landslide risk management starts with a better understanding of the nature and magnitude of the risks faced. This involves mapping and analysis of where and when a landslide is likely to occur, the potential volume and extent, what and who is exposed, and the potential impacts on people and key infrastructure. This atlas provides a comprehensive set of maps to support this risk analysis and make it possible to identify the most vulnerable slopes, communities, and infrastructure that require urgent attention in terms of monitoring and mitigation.

It is also essential to continuously monitor landslide risks, including in real time. Lower-cost and community-supported solutions are available and have proved sustainable. Recent years have also seen significant advances in automated satellite-based and remote sensing mapping and monitoring technologies as a complement to field-based monitoring.

There is no single solution to reduce landslide hazards. As demonstrated by the Ayusai case study, an integrated package of measures is likely to be most efficient and effective. Measures should be tailored to the specific needs and conditions of each site, based on comprehensive studies. Mitigating landslide risk can draw on a combination of structural and nonstructural measures, such as the unloading and reshaping of slopes, improved surface water drainage and spring catchment, and the creation of protective structures, including nature-based retainers. These measures can be complemented by regreening, monitoring and early warning systems, small-scale resettlement, and community awareness-raising and preparedness actions.

Integrated landslide risk management requires a solid policy and governance framework. It should have well-defined priorities, mandates, and procedures to ensure an all-of-government and all-of-society approach to reducing risk and building resilience. The Kyrgyz Republic needs improved capacities, standards, and procedures related to risk assessment, monitoring and early warning, physical mitigation, nature-based solutions, risk-informed land use planning, insurance, and resettlement. It will be essential to affirm and enhance the role of communities and local authorities in monitoring, reducing, and preparing for landslide risk.

Under the Landslide Risk Management Sector Project, ADB is supporting the Kyrgyz Republic to improve its systems and capacities for landslide risk reduction and monitoring (footnote 75). The project combines engineering and nature-based solutions with community-based planning and capacity-building for sustainable long-term landslide safety. The project will reduce the landslide risks to infrastructure, community assets, and livelihoods in selected sites by implementing risk mitigation engineering measures such as unloading, reshaping of bulging or cracked areas, and drainage of underground and surface water. The design and planning will include community consultations, with an emphasis on the participation of women and women-headed households. Nature-based solutions will be incorporated where suitable.

The project will also modernize and strengthen the institutional capacities of MES and other local stakeholders in landslide risk monitoring. An integrated multi-level landslide monitoring system will be established, combining on-site monitoring as well as a pilot national-level satellite-based landslide monitoring system incorporating Interferometric Synthetic Aperture Radar (InSAR). On-site monitoring systems will be installed in about 20 sites, and will comprise sensors to measure slope stability, groundwater levels, and key trigger variables. The pilot InSAR system will provide enable broad-based monitoring of surface displacements and analysis of historical slope stability, and support updating of the national landslide inventory. The integrated system will be linked to the existing national early warning system and the national call center and network of crisis management centers.

The project will strengthen the procedures and capacities of government agencies, local authorities, and communities on multi-hazard risk assessment and mapping; monitoring; community risk assessment and planning; gender; and landslide risk mitigation, including resettlement. The project will establish a geographic information system-based landslide risk assessment platform and database integrating information on landslide hazard, exposure, and vulnerability. This platform will support selection and analysis of risk mitigation interventions under the project.

This project, along with other initiatives, will help reduce fatalities, injuries, and direct and indirect economic losses from landslides in the most vulnerable communities in the Kyrgyz Republic.